The cultural dimension of development:
towards a practical approach

The cultural dimension of development

Towards a practical approach

Culture and development series

UNESCO Publishing

The authors are responsible for the choice and
the presentation of the facts contained in this
book and for the opinions expressed therein,
which are not necessarily those of UNESCO
and do not commit the Organization.

Published in 1995 by the United Nations Educational,
Scientific and Cultural Organization
7, place de Fontenoy, 75352 Paris 07 SP

Composed by Susanne Almeida-Klein
Printed by Imprimerie de la Manutention, 53100 Mayenne

ISBN 92-3-103043-4

Preface

This methodological review produced by UNESCO is the fruit of a process going back more than ten years. It began at the Mexico Conference on Cultural Policies, which recommended that a World Decade for Cultural Development be jointly sponsored by the United Nations and UNESCO. The first objective for this Decade is to 'Acknowledge the cultural dimension in development', and the conference made it clear that since '. . . culture constitutes a fundamental part of the life of each individual and of each community . . . consequently, development – whose ultimate aim should be focused on man – must have a cultural dimension'. The terms 'fundamental', 'ultimate aim' and 'must' indicate sufficiently that, while culture is an element of development, it is not just one factor among others, but the very basis of development, its driving force and final horizon.

It was on that foundation that UNESCO's activities in this field were based in the 1980s, as were some of the initiatives taken since 1988 and which were specific to the Decade. The first stage in its work was to reflect on the meaning and implications of the subject, and particularly its descriptive and normative character. The fact is that culture is present in all development activity, and this truth – once it is acknowledged that human beings in all their diversity are the real object of development – has to be taken into account in development strategies, plans and projects.

Apart from stating these principles, UNESCO's action has concentrated on two main objectives, firstly to ensure that taking cultural factors and effects into account in development really does become a shared task for the institutions of the United Nations system, and secondly to monitor and analyse the extent to which this is being done in development projects, particularly at the local level where it may most easily be shown to be present.

Developing co-ordination among the United Nations institutions was a very gradual process. It was the subject of inter-organization meetings in the framework of the United Nations Administration and Co-ordination Committee and was accompanied by joint activities, meetings and projects between UNESCO and certain specialized United Nations institutions, as will be seen in Part One of this book. Furthermore, through the contacts made on these various occasions and the information gathered for the purposes of this review, it was possible to discern the similarity in the initiatives and concerns of the various institutions involved. In their different ways, they have produced an analysis of the shortcomings in thought and action on development to date and made efforts to create and experiment with appropriate methodological instruments, enabling them to improve the way they designed and carried out their programmes and projects. In addition, over the same period, the international scientific community has conducted a parallel set of studies and research projects which led to the same doubts and the same conclusions. Lastly, the strongest claim for another type of development, and therefore for different methods and approaches, came from the field, often thanks to the non-governmental organizations (NGOs).

For its part, UNESCO had a series of case-studies carried out on local development projects during the 1980s which led to some interesting findings. In particular this work showed that the cultural characteristics of a particular milieu are only perceived as obstacles in a purely 'economicist' approach. On the contrary, they may, as shown by much analytical work both in UNESCO and elsewhere, be the most dynamic factor in certain projects with which the populations concerned identify themselves.

This assumes, however, that these facts are fully taken on board and accepted and that the people take an active part in planned or present development projects.

This idea, which gradually attracted a growing consensus, directly raises the question of the approach, ways and means and – it might be added – pedagogics of development. This question, central to the Decade, is also raised – and partly answered – by the international development organizations. It is asked, too, in the form of a request for measuring instruments – otherwise called cultural development indicators – by development economists, managers and planners. Lastly, workers in the field also seek guidance for the activity they are carrying out in direct contact with the populations or alongside the sponsoring authorities and financing institutions.

It was for this reason that UNESCO decided that its contribution to the World Decade for Cultural Development would be to devote a programme of work to questions of method. The programme, beginning with a phase of methodological study (this book being one of its products) will continue in 1994–95 with a phase of experimental application, ending in 1996–97 with the progressive application at international level of the instruments produced and tested.

Here we have to qualify the definition of the subject. Working out methods for taking the cultural dimension into account in development could appear to reflect a rather presumptuous attitude – particularly in the light of this volume's subtitle, 'Towards a practical approach'.

We know very well that there is no single and unified method for taking the cultural dimension into account in development because of the complexity of the subject and the importance of such things as diversity, interactions in the setting of the elements of the problem, to say nothing of the limits of a purely technical approach. Hence the need to put forward a spectrum of strategies, methods and instruments whose preferred use will depend on the type of situation considered, for example for high-level programming decisions or those taken at field level.

We also know that cultural reality, understood in the broad sense of lifestyles and ways of thinking and acting, knowledge and know-how and value systems, is difficult to reduce to abstract parameters which would 'kill' the reality they are supposed to describe. Exercises in quantification are therefore all the more difficult to use.

We know, too, that the concept of development carries with it a particular culture, namely that of the industrialized market economy countries, and it also infers its own models of behaviour and thought and its own value systems. We also know that each culture is split by conflicts and tensions between the groups making up its society and that it cannot, therefore, claim to be a unified and unalterable reality.

Lastly, discussion of development must include underdevelopment, poverty, violence and the many wars all round the world unceasingly facing the United Nations with new challenges.

But we would be untrue to our principles, approaches and our resolve to act if all we did was list the difficulties that UNESCO attempts to come to grips with in this methodological study: the nature of the relations between macro- and micro-economic levels, the lack of communication between centres of decision and the field, quantification of data and training in the cultural approach to development and building up general awareness of that approach.

On that basis, this document puts forward a number of methods of analysis, programming and evaluation for major development authorities, covering not only the formulation of terms of reference for projects but also ways and means of implementing and evaluating them. It also tackles the feasibility problems of cultural development pedagogics and opens the vital debate on participation.

This work will therefore go hand in hand with the drawing-up of technical documents for planners and also the writing-up of one or more practical guides for fieldworkers.

The various documents will, of course, be tested, made more precise, amplified or even modified as a result of experimental application in projects where this approach and these resources may be calculated to enable action that is taken to be enriched and made more suitable.

So the working method used in this project is wholly pragmatic. It gives and will continue to give full scope, firstly to existing knowledge and secondly to the sometimes difficult yet irreplaceable experience of those working in the field. However, since the questions dealt with are scientifically complex, the process of carrying out the exercise will, from start to finish, call heavily on the work of development specialists. All in all, UNESCO's contribution to the common task of all who are working for more humane development will be a set of working instruments that are scientifically credible but intended for practitioners.

Contents

Foreword

The concept of development as a more or less linear series of changes, proceeding from primitive to other more sophisticated methods of production and from everyday hardships to a more comfortable life by means of technological improvements, is a relatively recent notion. No such idea existed in the Middle Ages.

It is also a very Western concept. It is intimately linked to the modern industrialization process, since it is through mass production and mass communication that it has become possible to raise the standard of living of the majority of ordinary people. In most Third World countries the whole notion of development is still alien to cultural traditions as it used to be alien to Europeans a few hundred years ago.

Modern development can be said to have started, ideologically, during the Age of the Enlightenment. It became very tangible during the Industrial Revolution. It is to a very large extent a product of capitalism, yet it was inherited without major change by Marxist socialism.

It is interesting to see that both capitalism and socialism have been basically acultural in their approach to development processes. Liberal capitalism in its purest form tends to consider development processes as universal: things progress as a result of scientific discoveries and according to the laws of the market. In principle, attempts to intervene politically or otherwise are likely simply to disturb the process and generate problems.

Socialism in its Marxist form also considered that the principles according to which development should be pursued were scientifically determined and universal. Hence, there was no real difference

11

between developing a well-to-do European country, a nomadic central Asian province or a poor tropical island state. Evoking cultural differences when discussing economic and social development was for long considered a reactionary or revisionist deviation. Although popular cultural expressions have often been tolerated, they have been obliged to appear as an ornamental 'folkloric' element only.

Against this background, it is easy to understand why development co-operation, in both its bilateral and its multilateral form, has neglected the cultural dimension of development. Four development decades have been declared by the United Nations, the fourth having started in 1991. As experience has accumulated over the years, the approach has been gradually modified. United Nations agencies and bilateral donor agencies no longer commit the same type of basic, flagrant errors in implementing development projects as they did at the start. The need for human resource development has been widely recognized: so too has the important role of women in development. And with the Rio Summit on Development and the Environment in 1992, the notion of environmentally sustainable development has become generally accepted, if not always respected.

And yet there is one important imponderable which is decisive in the development process and which has yet to gain general recognition. It has to do with the collective motivation of a people or community, and this motivation is to a large extent culturally determined. It is this collective motivation that has to be mobilized if a development programme is to achieve more than mere economic growth and modernization.

To be a true contribution to a country's development, external assistance must aim at producing multiplier effects and make the development process become the direct concern of the target group. If this is to be made possible, those who plan and those who take decisions on development programmes must necessarily try to understand what cultural obstacles they may encounter, what the driving forces are in the society concerned and how to strike the right chords in its cultural 'subconscious. If and when that is done, even a limited initial investment may produce important multiplier effects.

But when this is recognized, the question remains: How do we take the cultural dimension of development into account in a concrete situation? Where is the know-how, what are the instruments, how do we transform the general recognition that this is important into useful practical advice? This remains one of the most important tasks that the World Decade for Cultural Development has set out to solve and this book constitutes a first step in that direction.

The main objective of the World Decade for Cultural Development (1988–97), which is the most concrete result of the World Conference on Cultural Policies, held in Mexico City in 1982, is to promote 'the acknowledgement of the cultural dimension of development'. The time has come for us to recognize that development (and actions which aspire to contribute to development) can never be reduced to a simple question of technical solutions and financial calculations.

It is also generally recognized that psychic factors are often decisive in the process of curing a patient of a serious somatic disease. What is true for individuals is also true for groups of individuals, that is, communities great and small. It is time that it was recognized that development requires a similar sort of collective motivation in order to take off. Development takes place at the interface between hard facts (such as technological inventions and financial decisions) on the one hand and non-tangible factors such as collective dreams, aspirations, pride, inventiveness, taboos, fears, etc., on the other.

This is a field of which there can be no exact knowledge. As in the field of pedagogy, the interplay of all relevant factors that may influence the process is far too complex to allow for any fail-safe rules. But that does not mean that nothing can ever be learned or taught about these factors. In the pedagogic field we know quite a lot, since the field has been under study for a long time and lots of resources have gone into research. This is not yet the case for development, which is a relatively new subject area.

This book represents a significant step towards developing some basic knowledge about the cultural factors that condition development. It is an attempt at a state-of-the-art presentation based on experience gained both inside and outside the United Nations system, as well as a first outline of a possible methodology for integrating the cultural dimension into development programmes and projects.

ANDERS ARFWEDSON
World Decade for Cultural Development
UNESCO

13

Acknowledgements

This document was drafted by Claude Fabrizio with the assistance of Dominique Desjeux and Xavier Dupuis, particularly in Parts Two and Three, under the direction of Máté Kovács.

It also takes account of studies carried out by Djamchid Behnam, Bernard Clergerie, Henry Panhuys, Edith Sizoo and Thierry Verhelst, and the findings of documentary exploration by Louis Augustin-Jean and Amaury Faivre d'Arcier.

Luce Kellermann was consulted too, as were Winfried Böll, Jean-Pierre Boyer, Daniel Etounga-Manguele, Bernard Gosset and Paul-Marc Henry.

We wish to thank for their support not only those mentioned above, but also the organizations that replied to the survey carried out as part of the preparatory work for this document, and in particular the Canadian International Development Agency (CIDA).

'Development cannot be limited to economic growth only. It also embraces a political, social, human and environmental as well as cultural dimension.'

Introduction

The guinea-pig and the 'developer'[1]

As has often been said, the identification of cultural factors in development – and the negative effects of their underestimation on the sought-after results – are nowhere so clearly seen as on the ground, even when they are the result of government decisions or of the intervention of the relevant international institutions. This is why it was felt useful – before launching into a more general and therefore more abstract (in appearance anyway) review – to begin with a true story which has the flavour and educational impact of a fable.

In this connection, it may be useful to point out that the use of quotation marks around the word 'developer' in the above heading and around the word 'developed' from time to time in the study is intentional and designed to show the artificial nature of such a demarcation still to be found too often among people who are really partners: the development workers and the general population involved in projects for which they should always be co-responsible.

Early in the 1980s, the Ecuadorian Ministry of Agriculture decided to launch a guinea-pig farming project with the financial help of the World Bank. The objective was a classic one: to take a traditional agricultural activity, the raising of guinea-pigs, which

1. From the article by E. P. Archetti, 'An Anthropological Perspective on Cultural Change and Development: A Case-study from the Highlands of Ecuador', quoted by D. Desjeux in *Le sens de l'autre* [Awareness of Others], pp. 21–6, Paris, UNESCO/ICA, 1991.

17

goes back well before the Spanish conquest, and try to modernize it. The basic arguments were twofold: the guinea-pig is an important feature of the rural population's diet and the urban market is potentially large. So the aim of the project was to increase agricultural production of guinea-pigs. For this purpose a 'rational' farming strategy was proposed, but it was to be applied in the context of the Ecuadorian peasant 'culture' of the high plateaux.

Following the specialists' rational analysis of the problem, the diagnosis was as follows:

Guinea-pigs are traditionally raised in the home and more specifically in peasant kitchens. Little control is exercised and feeding is a matter of luck: the guinea-pigs eat what is left of the day's cooking. There is no systematic inspection for disease, and treatment is often given too late. Productivity is badly restricted by the traditional way the guinea-pigs are raised, which, in other words, is quite irrational. This is an obstacle to the changes it would be desirable to make to the Ecuadorian agricultural economy.

The technical solution proposed was therefore as follows:

The animals should be kept outside the kitchen and the peasants' living area in new cages designed so as to keep the sexes apart and for better control of rearing methods and of diseases that were decimating the numbers of guinea-pigs. There should be genetic control of males and females to prevent degeneration of the species. New species should be introduced. Better and more rational feed should be provided, lucerne being considered the best. A leaflet on ways of maintaining the best possible health conditions would be produced.

These proposals could bring nothing but good. The technical solutions advanced are rational: their dissemination should not pose any problem except for ill-will on the part of the peasants or their possibly over-traditional mentality. It would be simply a matter of teaching them how to go about things. Lastly, showing them how the scheme would work and the economic benefit it would bring would be enough to motivate them to learn the techniques. Thus the project had all the appearances of agronomic, institutional and economic relevance and rationality.

This, however, is where the cultural dimension of the problem assumes its full importance.

The point of view of the technicians was to see the guinea-pigs as food, consumed primarily for its nutritional value, and not as a foodstuff with special cultural significance. A cultural approach to the situation shows, on the contrary, that the social and symbolic significance of the guinea-pig is greater than its market or even nutritional value. The guinea-pig is an exceptional foodstuff. Its consumption is tied in with the stages in the family cycle at its most important moments (birth, baptism, first communion, confirmation, marriage, birthdays and death) and with social events, particularly those in which the intention is to show regard for friends, neighbours, 'godparents', natural parents and any authority or persons of importance.

It is also bound up with civil and religious festivals: religious ceremonies and pilgrimages and important civil ceremonies. Last of all, the guinea-pig is used as a way of treating pneumonia, bronchitis and colds. During pregnancy, a woman should eat guinea-pig frequently, as she should also from one week after the birth of the child for a period of three months, preferably in soup. There is a link between the presence of the guinea-pig near the oven in the kitchen and the happiness of the family. So its presence in the home is essential.

The conclusion to be drawn from this story is that it is not possible to forgo a cultural study if a development project, however technically well designed it may be, is to avoid the possibility of failure. From the very beginning, therefore, an anthropologist has to be called upon to make a study of the whole cultural environment of the project.

This apparent irrationality is not the preserve of the Third World or of the peasantry. Recourse to elucidation techniques helps the development worker firstly to gain awareness of the culture in which he is working and secondly to understand that certain mechanisms that he discovers in others also exist in his own case. Techniques therefore have to be invented or adapted enabling the situation or the rules of the game to be changed – which compels the players to adjust to the new situation – or making it possible for the know-how the players already have to be mobilized, one way being via their social networks.

Aim and general context of the review – brief historical background

Culture and development: the fundamentally heterogeneous nature of these two concepts has long been stressed. Culture was considered to be both the perfect expression of a society and the sum of its history, a more or less timeless foundation on which everything was based: in other words a society's heritage and creativity primarily in its artistic and literary forms. Development, on the other hand, was the result of the transformation of Western societies, beginning in the early nineteenth century, under the combined impact of economic liberalism and scientific and technological progress, the latter being regarded as its systematic application and most remarkable product.

It was only towards the end of the nineteenth century that the problem of the cultural and social cost of economic and technical progress, and, much more recently, that of the violent or non-violent encounter between this progress and the different – and more particularly non-European – cultures because of the very rapid improvements in transport facilities, first came to be posed, though without any link being established between the two.

These changes coincided with the revival of colonial expansion and the radical challenge to liberal economics by socialist theories based on centralized planning and the state economy. Apart from these two principles, socialism, as applied firstly in the Soviet Union and secondly, after the Second World War, in Eastern Europe and various other countries elsewhere in the world, was also based on scientific progress and economic growth, particularly in heavy industry, as the engine of development.

It needed decolonization for the problem of the economic autonomy of the newly independent countries to surface and to be answered in terms of development. The affirmation of the cultural identities of the infant nations went hand in hand with that aspiration. It was largely within the context of the intergovernmental conferences on cultural policies organized by UNESCO that the two terms 'culture' and 'development' were first linked and the question of the cultural dimension of development first raised. This line of thinking, coinciding with more intensive scientific study of development, culminated in the 1982 World Conference on Cultural Policies (MONDIACULT) held in Mexico City, where the concepts and definitions of culture, development and the cultural dimension of development on which this study is based were formulated.

Before embarking on a closer examination of our subject, it is worth recalling the wording of these concepts and definitions. Doubtless there are those who, for one reason or another, would prefer to use others. However, to avoid a debate on the advantages and disadvantages of the various possible formulae, we have chosen the definitions on which UNESCO's activities in this field are founded.

They are, what is more, the fruit of a long process of reflection and consultation on the part of the Member States during the 1970s and 1980s within the framework of various regional conferences on cultural policies organized by UNESCO and, though capable of improvement, have shown themselves to be useful tools for tackling the problems of the cultural dimension of development.

What is meant by the cultural dimension of development?

The concept of the cultural dimension of development has evolved considerably. Thus, during the 1980s, there was a transition from the idea of cultural dimension to that of the factors, parameters and cultural impact of development. Conversely, culture was no longer defined as a subsidiary or even ornamental dimension of development but as the very fabric of society in its overall relation with development and as the internal force of that society.

It is in these terms that the definition adopted by the Mexico City Conference should be understood. According to this approach, the cultural dimension of development embraces all the psycho-sociological components which, like the economic, technological and scientific factors, help to improve the material and intellectual life of the populations without introducing any violent change into their way of life or modes of thought, and at the same time contribute to the technical success of the development plans or projects.

Balanced development can only be ensured by making cultural factors an integral part of the strategies designed to achieve it; consequently, these strategies should always be devised in the light of the historical, social and cultural context of each society.[2]

The cultural factors should be taken into account at the project planning stage, when they may either act as constraints, slowing down development, or serve to stimulate social change. They should also be borne in mind when evaluating action to bring about economic and social change where sociocultural impact has to be assessed.

To grasp the full meaning of this definition of the cultural dimension of development and the ways in which it can be taken into account, it must be amplified by a reminder of the definitions of culture and development adopted by the Mexico Conference, because the definition of the cultural dimension of development itself stems from those definitions.

During the 1960s and 1970s, the concept of 'culture', frequently still restricted to its products, in particular works of art and literature and the cultural heritage in the form of both objects and buildings, was progressively extended to give rise to the notion of cultural development and, around 1975, to that of the cultural dimension of development.

Since the World Conference on Cultural Policies (Mexico City, 1982), it is recognized that culture is 'the whole complex of distinctive spiritual, material, intellectual and emotional features that characterize a society or social group. It includes not only the arts and letters, but also modes of life, the fundamental rights of the human being, value systems, traditions and beliefs'.[3] However, this definition, whose main quality lies in its globality, has certain limitations: it does not completely explain the dynamic nature of every culture, or the exchanges and interchanges between cultures. Nor does it pay sufficient heed to the evolution that all cultures go through, firstly because of their own dynamic and secondly because they come under the influence of all kinds of globalization, modernization and technological, economic and social transformation processes.

2. UNESCO, *Mexico City Declaration on Cultural Policies,* Article 16 (final report of Mondiacult: World Conference on Cultural Policies, Mexico City, 26 July to 6 August 1982), Paris, UNESCO, 1982. (UNESCO doc. CLT/MD/1.)
3. UNESCO, op. cit., Preamble.

The definition of development is more difficult to find if all its various uses are to be covered.

The definition adopted by the Mexico City Conference sets a relative standard. The final report states that development is 'a complex, comprehensive and multidimensional process which extends beyond mere economic growth to incorporate all dimensions of life and all the energies of a community, all of whose members are called upon to make a contribution and can expect to share in the benefits'. Thus, it establishes the principle that 'development should be based on the will of each society and should express its fundamental identity'.[4]

In fact, only a broad, anthropological conception of culture can provide the necessary basis for its description and its correlation with development. No less important, from both the theoretical and operational standpoints, is the need to take into account the complex, comprehensive and multidimensional nature of development. This acceptation of the term leads to the adoption of a systemic approach to the analysis of the transformation processes in every field, giving particular attention to the cultural dynamic and the question of the interactions between culture and development.

The definition also implies that human beings are the agents and beneficiaries of development and that the latter can be fully encompassed, in all its aspects, only within the context of an integrative approach. Finally, it leads, as we have seen, to the notion of the cultural dimension of development, which records a fact, sets a requirement and reminds us that the incorporation of cultural data in strategies aimed at achieving balanced economic and social development is one of the essential conditions for success, to the extent that it is based upon the real cultural life of all human communities.

General framework and main thrust of the study

The definitions adopted at the Mexico City Conference reflect the international community's recognition, in principle, of the need to go beyond the purely economic view of development and to include cultural factors among the diverse components of development seen

4. UNESCO, op. cit., Preamble and Articles 10 to 16.

as a multidimensional process. It must, however, be admitted that, despite the advances made in the 1980s, the principle is still far from being universally applied.

This slowness to respond to changes in approach can be partly attributed to difficulties of a theoretical and practical nature. It is also ascribable to a relative lack of political will, either because the new approach implies a radical upheaval in modes of thought and behaviour or because it might conflict with domestic or external economic or even political strategies.

DEVELOPMENT – A CYCLICAL, POLYMORPHOUS AND UNEQUAL PHENOMENON

Involving, as it does, an international approach to the problems of development, the present study needs to be placed in the context of the persistent economic, social and cultural crisis affecting the countries of the South as well as the industrialized countries, including those making the transition to democracy and a market economy.

Thus, it is first necessary to examine the above-mentioned definition of development in conjunction with the complementary notions of underdevelopment, misdevelopment and 'alternative' development. These notions have their origin in the practical problems and shortcomings of the purely economic approach to development, in the countries of the North as well as of the South. However, as we shall see, even at this stage it is imperative to differentiate.

The notion of underdevelopment implies a certain backwardness relative to the model constituted by the industrial societies, if the improvement of the living conditions of the people is assumed to depend predominantly on economic performance. The term 'least developed countries' is also one whose currency derives from the use of purely economic criteria. As we shall see, this excessively narrow thinking is being increasingly questioned, in particular within the United Nations system. In another light, some researchers have analysed the relationship between industrialized and developing countries in terms of 'centre' and 'periphery' or on the basis of the situations of dependence of the countries of the South on those of the North.[5]

---

5.   For example, A. Mattelart, *International Image Markets in Search of an Alternative Perspective,* London, Comedia, 1989.

However this may be, the bundling together of all the countries of the South in the category 'developing countries' no longer corresponds to reality. Between the economically less advanced and the industrial countries there lies a steadily expanding group of countries which have embarked on the development process without, for all that, having rejected or destroyed their own culture, in some of its aspects at least. The example of the countries of East Asia is particularly instructive in this respect.[6]

Misdevelopment is the term sometimes used to describe the distortions which the crude application of the purely economicist, i.e. management, model in the industrialized nations can introduce, not only in the social and cultural areas but even in the economy itself.

Here again, however, the concept is too general to permit the indispensable distinction to be made between the situation of the 'Western' countries and that of the former socialist states.

The strictly economic development model originated in the Western countries, where it still operates as a 'super-standard', despite the emergence of opposition movements that seek to ensure development by less costly means in social, ecological and human terms, especially in view of the recent aggravation of the employment crisis in Europe. The same quest for an economic and social development model inspires the current debate in the developing countries, which are considering how they might consolidate and bring under control the means of improving their situation.

The primacy of strictly economic calculations and short-term profitability over consideration for the human and social costs is, for some, the mark of misdevelopment, whose effects are now becoming increasingly apparent. Misdevelopment is characterized by poverty, unemployment, the exclusion of certain social groups or cultural minorities, the dehumanization of the urban environment, rural depopulation, and the ghettoization of the suburbs or, in North America, town centres. Another of its consequences is the emergence of 'non-conforming' urban subcultures, with marginalization, disregard for dominant values and fascination for certain technological innovations, and which appear and disappear with great rapidity.

6. S. H. K. Yeh, *Understanding Development: Modernization and Cultural Values in Asia and the Pacific Region*, Paris, UNESCO, 1989. (UNESCO doc. STY.89.)

In the former socialist states, on the other hand, the incorporation of the cultural dimension in development primarily involves the identification of the cultural conditions and effects of the passage to democracy and a market economy. After decades of repression of identity resulting from the monolithism of the previous political system, it is important not to sacrifice the surviving features of the national culture in the process of creating new cultural, economic and political models which take into account the scale of the changes now in progress and the extent of the adaptation necessary after discarding the model of the centrally planned economy.

As regards the transition to democracy, the understanding and recognition of cultural plurality and intercultural contacts, the cultural factors to be taken into account first and foremost in development projects are those relating to the process of familiarization with the notions of participation and dialogue.

As far as the transition to a market economy is concerned, familiarization with private initiative and the spirit of free enterprise and a readiness to fend for oneself, in the framework of generally accepted rules, are the essential ingredients.

THE CHALLENGES OF DEVELOPMENT

The complexity of the problem does not derive solely from the more or less relative applicability of the major concepts adopted for the purpose of this study. It is equally bound up with the scale of the challenges facing the international community and the institutions and officials responsible for the search for 'development with a human face'. Finally, it is also connected with the worldwide nature of the problems of development and the large number of their dimensions: cultural, economic, technological and political in the proper sense. It is in this light that the great challenges of development, present and future, should be viewed.

These difficulties confront the world with a series of challenges whose scale will define priorities for action and determine the ability of international co-operation to respond. In any event, the response will require that development be treated as a comprehensive and multidimensional process and that its cultural dimension be fully taken into account, both as a contributory factor and as a body of positive and negative effects that need to be thoroughly understood. However, as we shall see, a series of changes is taking place, making the solution of the problems of development a matter of some urgency: How can the harsh realities of the market-place be reconciled by reference to traditional cultures? It is a problem whose eventual solution will have profound and enduring effects.

Global population trends are one of the basic ingredients of development problems at world level.

Without considering in detail the trends of the last twenty years or the demographers' predictions, we propose merely to draw certain conclusions concerning development and its cultural dimension and impact:

- the growth of the world population will make it increasingly necessary to give priority to the problems of economic and social development and to take into account the non-economic, particularly cultural, factors as accelerators of or obstacles to the growth of production and the balanced distribution of the goods and resources essential to the intellectual and spiritual – as well as physiological – life of all humanity;
- the constant growth of the urban population has an obvious cultural dimension in so far as living conditions, employment and family and social life are concerned, while the city supports a culture that can destabilize new arrivals with different backgrounds and hasten the break-up of the traditional extended family and even the nuclear family itself;
- the rapid increase in the numbers of young people (up to 24 years of age), particularly in the developing countries (in spite of the recent world trend for populations to age), is also having an impact on the cultural dimension of development, to the extent that it raises questions concerning the culture of origin as opposed to the educational culture, the transition from school to work, the preservation of family cohesion, and the search for motivational values other than the material values of which the contribution of the modern world sometimes seems to consist.

The persistently high rates of population growth in the developing countries and the increasing proportions of young people and city dwellers are decisive indicators of the future trend as far as the problems of international development are concerned.

In particular, these indicators should be compared with those on the growth of world production of goods and services, if reference is made to the strategy employed by the International Labour Organization (ILO) for meeting basic needs, and with the exploitation of natural resources, where resource management and the preservation of the natural environment, necessary as it is to the man–nature ecosystem, are at stake.

The Brundtland Report, *Our Common Future*, presented at the United Nations Assembly during its 42nd Ordinary Session, added that 'the bringing into relationship of the figures on world population and the resource production required to satisfy the "basic needs" of all and effectively combat poverty also leads to the formulation of the problem of family size, as a means of ensuring that women are able to exercise their fundamental rights to self-determination', both in family matters and in the fields of education and work.

Without doubt, the possibilities and conditions that will help to bring about a significant improvement in all these various situations include taking into consideration the questions at issue and the cultural impact of any remedial action taken, preferably within the context of integrated development strategies or projects.

The economic challenges can be fully understood only in relation to the demographic challenge outlined above. The preceding considerations already make it necessary to mention the conditions of growth in the production and distribution of goods and services for the benefit of all the world's populations. What is more, all countries should be able to secure access to the international trade circuit. On all these points, unfortunately, an examination of international economic trends is not encouraging.

In fact, it is worth recalling some of the main observations incorporated in the third *Human Development Report* (1992) by the United Nations Development Programme (UNDP), which reformulate the problem of the relations between economic growth and human development or, in other words, between the improvement in living conditions and the tempering of the negative aspects of economic expansion:

(i) Economic growth does not automatically lead to an improvement in individual living conditions at national or international level. The poorer socio-economic groups and countries have limited access to credit, capital, and the most efficient techniques and means of production, whence their indebtedness and the development of the informal sector.

(ii) Rich countries and poor countries have very unequal access to the world market. The latter are unable to export their products freely, since the world markets are in the hands of the big industrialized countries, especially as regards raw materials and high-added-value products.

As a result of this situation, many developing countries have seen their market access restricted and their terms of trade deteriorate. These countries, especially the least advanced and most deeply indebted among them, can no longer repay their debt and are therefore obliged to implement structural adjustment policies which, if not accompanied by investment in the productive and job-creating sectors, weigh most heavily on the underprivileged and may provoke serious social unrest.

Consequently, basic needs may not always be satisfied and problems of employment, especially among the young, may assume alarming proportions. Essentially the only means of escape from this type of situation is mass emigration to the industrialized countries, whose welcome is wearing increasingly thin as the economic crisis begins to bite. For the populations left behind, the daily struggle for the basic necessities means that survival strategies have to be found and poverty cultures emerge that may reveal unsuspected capacities to resist, except in situations where the deprivation is total.

However, this statement needs to be qualified to the extent that examples of rapid economic take-off, which so far do not appear to conflict seriously with the values and cultures of the peoples concerned, are to be found in a number of countries of South-East Asia and the Far East, including China. On the other hand, it should not be forgotten that the rift between development and underdevelopment may sometimes be encountered within the borders of a single country, for example in certain countries of Latin America. Finally, even among the industrialized countries themselves, there is a sharp division between the Western countries and those of Eastern Europe.

In every case, the presence of a culture imbued with dynamic values and the adaptation of model social and economic development strategies to the culture, values and mentality of the community or country concerned are necessary stages on the road to development. Without them, education, health and family economic policies and projects cannot succeed, nor can the conditions of access to information and new technologies improve.

The existence of major cultural challenges is another important aspect of the present world situation. Clearly, cultures are not carved in stone: values, ways of life, traditions and beliefs are shaken by the impact of development in the economic sense. However, like economic life, they are also influenced by other cultures and especially by cultural trends on the world scale. At the same time, the great challenges of society overlap into the cultural domain, transforming its previous configuration and redefining its limits.

These two tendencies directly involve the question of the cultural dimension of development at world level, especially as regards the design and effects of development programmes and strategies. They can therefore be described as major cultural trends and should figure in any global scenario that attempts to depict the interaction between culture and development.

THE SCIENTIFIC AND TECHNOLOGICAL CHALLENGES

From the start of the century and particularly since the second post-war period, the striking feature of scientific progress has been the great advance in knowledge and the ever-increasing spread of applications in the various technologies. All the techniques now in use represent opportunities to solve many of the problems facing mankind: improving agricultural production, health, new clothing and building materials, cultural 'machines' such as radio and television receivers, biotechnologies, genetics, new data storage, processing and dissemination techniques and robotization of some forms of industrial production.

But these innovations, positive in themselves, raise a number of economic, political, cultural and ethical problems all of whose consequences and implications have not yet, perhaps, been assessed.

A first and major problem for the whole of mankind is the impossibility of taking an all-embracing view of scientific progress, but it is above all the technical fallout from scientific discoveries that causes what are often unforeseeable difficulties. The improvement in the productivity of certain branches of industry or agriculture, for example, is responsible for drastic reductions in employment opportunities, particularly in the industrial countries, and is creating a profound moral and cultural crisis, particularly among young people.

The vast potential for the dissemination of information by the media, TV and radio in particular, or by the tremendous international development in the computer field and the now general interconnection of data centres, works in the direction of both the globalization of problems and the increasing elimination of what is specific or real-life and creates, particularly in the economic and financial field, a continuous strengthening of supranational strategies, particularly those of the big private-sector concerns.

Another and increasingly acute question is that of the ethical dimension in the development of the life sciences and in the scientific and technical field in general. The birth and growth of ethical committees in the various scientific and technical fields show clearly that the question of preserving the cultural and spiritual values that underlie the life of all societies and the invention of new values for the societies of the future concerns both those whose work it is to think and act in this field and scientific and technical specialists themselves.

But the quest for an answer to these challenges does not stop there. It also means introducing science and technology into the field of development as new cultural realities and, in particular, into the field of school and non-school education throughout the world – including, of course, other ways of producing and transmitting know-how as they have come into existence and spread, down the ages, in all the cultures of the world. In this regard there is no deep dilemma between modern Western forms of knowledge and the older forms developed in non-Western societies. Their existence and validity for thought and action too have to be considered in the general framework of the interaction between culture and development.

Lastly, given that the new scientific and technological advances are mainly produced by the industrialized countries, their gradual transfer as the need arises to all the countries that have not yet had sufficient access to them will be an instrument of crucial importance among all the teaching media for integrating the cultural dimension into development.

THE MAIN TRANSNATIONAL CULTURAL TRENDS

The main trends of cultural development operating on a world scale have transnational or multinational origins or reflect situations that can be encountered anywhere in the world or extend over huge

31

geographical areas embracing one or more continents. Thus, the evolution of the great religions, the worldwide adoption of certain cultural models, the expansion of some languages and the contraction of others, large-scale movements of population – economic migration, refugees, mass tourism – and the revival of nationalism and ethnicism, all these have a far-reaching influence on the problems of development.

Consider the evolution and geocultural spread of the great religions. Given the historically deep-rooted nature of cultural phenomena, one cannot but be struck by the steady migration of religions, notably Buddhism, Christianity and Islam, from one part of the world to another. A similarly noteworthy phenomenon is the rapid growth of more or less syncretic sects and cults. In this connection, the potential for conflict needs to be examined, together with the role that religious beliefs can play in promoting or restraining social solidarity, education and economic and social change.

Other important trends, often via the mass media, introduce new models of judgement and behaviour not necessarily adapted to the particular situation of the host population. This only makes it more difficult for people to shape the social and economic change for which they feel the need to their real aspirations, since they are ceaselessly bombarded with the image of an effortless prosperity through the mass dissemination of broad cultural messages which, furthermore, may weaken the diversity of cultures and lessen the chances of local creation.

Rapid advances in communications and information technology have facilitated the international circulation of these models, a mixed blessing with important consequences for the cultures of the less industrialized countries. On the one hand, it 'opens windows' on to the outside world in closed societies, as regards the exercise of democratic freedoms, for example, and, by the acquaintance it brings with other cultures, helps to relativize certain identities previously considered to be untouchable and to enrich life through contact with other human groups.

At the same time, the apologia for violence in the relations between peoples or individuals, the confusing of human with economic values and the widespread glorification of lifestyles inaccessible to the masses work powerfully against the establishment of development policies based on solidarity, self-confidence and long-term effort.

32

The same comments could be made about the increasingly extensive use of certain languages which, for reasons connected with international economic and political history, are spoken in places far removed from their cultural point of origin. Although this makes it easier for different populations to communicate, it simultaneously carries the risk of impoverishing the human cultural heritage, whose diversity is precisely one of its greatest assets.

The growth of the world's population is also leading to increased migration, from the countryside into the cities and from the countries of the South to those of the North, that is, from Latin America and the Caribbean to the United States, from Asia to Europe and North America, and from Africa to Europe. This migration is notable for the youthfulness of the migrants and their insistence on better living conditions in the host countries.

According to the Brundtland Report, 'migration from countryside to city is not in itself a bad thing'. The problem lies rather with the reduced possibilities for rural development and the growth of megalopolises where the mode of life exposes the newly arrived migrants to severe culture shock, even though it may flatter their hopes of better living conditions. The new forms of urbanization, born of the influx of migrants, pose often insurmountable human and cultural problems. But cases of cultural integration in towns are also observable in such situations (in Latin America, for example), and are due as much to the determination of the migrants as to the efforts of the social workers. Lastly, there is the forced migration of refugees caused by current conflicts in various parts of the globe.

The same applies to the migrants from the countries of the South to the industrial North. The transition from an often rural culture to a modern urban culture cannot be achieved without making strenuous efforts to adapt, though the difficulty lessens with succeeding generations. Solidarity among migrants is not always assured, and they also encounter housing conditions which represent the material form of the phenomena of sociocultural exclusion and marginalization. Migrants arriving in large numbers may also prompt reactions of xenophobia or even racism in the local people.

International migration may not be without its advantages for the migrant populations. These include the constitution of powerful diasporas in certain host countries, the transfer of capital back to the country of origin, and the return of migrants who then become agents of innovation, sometimes well – but sometimes not so well – received by their home community.

Among forms of international mobility, the tourism phenomenon is probably no smaller in scale. Moreover, tourism brings in hard currency, much appreciated by countries with an under-diversified economy, and creates jobs, directly and indirectly. At the same time, in certain social groups, in particular among the young, mass tourism, by its very nature, can breed dissatisfaction with the local culture and distort their view of the state of development of the country in which they live.

Both migration and tourism encourage a general trend towards the constitution of multicultural societies, with values and standards that may contradict or even conflict with each other.

At the same time, the spread of certain phenomena across the world does not have the same impact from one region to another. Moreover, cultural diversification is at work in many parts of the world. Finally, the pace of development is not the same in every field: whereas technologies and even ways of dressing and eating may change quickly, changes in cultural values are much slower to take effect. These differences in the pace of change result in transitional phases of variable duration and difficulty, which may generate tension and conflict.

Nevertheless, if the idea of the nation becomes part of the culture of a society at certain moments in history, it can in certain cases degenerate into nationalism and, even more so, ethnicism, a source of conflict which clearly rules out the slightest advance in development, whose indispensable preconditions are peace and solidarity.

In addition, the scale and pace of developments now taking place in terms of the growth of intercultural flows mask the situation of the cultural minorities of all types: minorities of different nationality in a given country, ethnocultural groups scattered over several countries and those minorities, often nomadic or representing the last vestiges of vanishing peoples, that oppose any integration into national political structures and modernity in general. Indeed, there is a convention concerning indigenous and tribal populations in independent countries which was adopted by the International Labour Conference (Geneva, 1989),[7] preserving their right to

7. International Labour Organization, *International Labour Conference,* Convention 169, Geneva, ILO, 1989.

refuse assimilation and to choose their own lifestyles and institutions and keep their own identities, languages and religions.

It also has to be said that, whereas, in the course of history, a return to an almost excessive affirmation of cultural identity almost always follows upon a phase in which different peoples come together to form a great multinational entity, notably during the colonial era, the present trend is to establish supranational entities on an economic basis, such as the European Union, the African Economic Union or the North Atlantic Free Trade Association (NAFTA) agreement linking the United States, Canada and Mexico, which is not without its cultural perspective.

CULTURE AND THE PROBLEMS OF SOCIETY

More and more, the cultural practices and values linked with modernization appear to be emerging as the 'cultural dimension' of the major problems of society in the contemporary world.

Thus, the environment is one of the new priorities that have recently come to the fore. Environmental issues are both a scientific reality and a new form of cultural value and attachment to the natural heritage, especially in urban and industrial societies. However, it should be noted that this is not the case in all those societies in which nature is considered sacred, in so far as it harbours forces both benevolent and harmful that affect the life of the people, and is regarded as a reservoir of natural resources (water, livestock, vegetation) whose consumption, which has now become unbalanced, previously allowed for the renewal of these resources.

In the field of health, problems such as AIDS and drug abuse clearly have, at least in part, a cultural origin and give rise to sub-cultures characterized by a marginal lifestyle and disregard for mainstream values. In this respect, they primarily affect the young and the uneducated and, even though they represent an objective danger, constitute a kind of indirect reaction to situations of economic, social and cultural adversity.[8]

Thus, the major trends of a new, transnational, urban, 'free-wheeling' culture, often borne along by the latest technologies, seem

8. World Health Organization, *The United Nations and Drug Abuse Control*, New York, United Nations, 1990; *AIDS and HIV Infection*, Geneva, WHO, 1991.

gradually to be taking shape. They find their strongest expression in the urban and peri-urban environment, where they coexist with less tragic but much more widespread forms of traumatism generated by everyday city life: stress, loneliness, anxiety and moral or mental 'drift'. But acculturation to urban values also acts as an apprenticeship to new concepts and gives access to complex development mechanisms.

Taken together, these practices, attitudes and critical experiences clearly form part of the general cultural problem of development, to the extent that they enter into violent opposition or positive interaction with the values of 'non-modernistic' societies. This may be the explanation for the movements to preserve ethical values, as a means of social cohesion and security, in Africa for example, or to perpetuate the observance of religious ceremonies and rituals, instances of which are to be found in many countries.

At the same time, the trend towards multiculturalism is bound to increase in strength, and the management of intercultural problems, therefore, must become a priority at world level. Thus, in the twenty-first century education and social and cultural action in all its forms will inevitably be faced with the challenge of how to enable all peoples belonging to different cultures to live amicably together. An important indicator in this regard will be the emergence of situations of cultural cross-breeding, as is already to be observed in often enriching but sometimes disconcerting forms, particularly in big towns.

So there is a close link between cultural problems and the problems of development: it is becoming ever clearer that the priorities in this field, far from being purely economic, also involve interpersonal communication, human dignity, and respect for other communities and their rules, standards and religion. These realities must be taken into account in devising new approaches – and the instruments for their implementation – aimed at incorporating cultural factors and effects into the theory and practice of development.

In the same way, it is in the light of the interactions between culture and development and of the great present and foreseeable demographic, economic, technological and cultural challenges, as previously defined, that new cultural development strategies need to be designed at national and international levels. In these strategies credible answers need to be presented, allowing for people's cultural practices and the growth of intercultural situations, with the object of forming new partnerships between institutional action and the private sector, with the participation of all communities and groups that might be given the initiative for local cultural development projects. Combined actions could thus be planned in which classic cultural activities, cultural industries, the media and new technologies could all be involved. Education in all its forms, mass sports, the environment, living conditions and, lastly, action for young people would all be an intrinsic part of these strategies which would, by definition, be multisectoral so as to be adaptable to the changes in progress in the field of cultural development seen as a particular aspect of the cultural dimension of development.

The basic facts

Following on from the above analysis it is essential, to ensure the credibility of any conclusions reached concerning the cultural dimension of development and the means of incorporating it into development assistance programmes and projects, to keep a number of basic facts clearly in mind:

- Cultures are not cast in stone: they have a past, a present and a future. Nor do they reflect a consensus, either within or between societies, but are manifestations of power. However, cultures are characterized not only by their diversity but also by their likenesses.
- Cultures are not 'intact' by reference to an original, more or less mythical, state: they are being continuously changed by contacts of all kinds between the various peoples and retain their primitive state solely in the case of certain minorities isolated by their activities from the trends occurring in the greater part of society. Conversely they are not to be defined solely as factors, but as the total expression of society in its non-functional aspects.
- Development is not simply the embodiment of economic progress, modernity, industrialization and science. It is, in at least equal measure, a question of human development, both individual and collective.
- Nor can development be regarded as a process of smooth, uninterrupted growth, always at work in the same regions of the globe. The economic crises which periodically beset the industrial societies are concrete evidence of this. At the same time

certain non-Western countries, sometimes while the industrial societies themselves are in crisis, may also launch themselves, rapidly or otherwise, into the development process and become significant partners in the world economy.

- These changes take place without apparent difficulty as regards the cultural acceptability of the predominantly economic development tools and strategies: profitability, market acquisition, massive deployment of science and new technologies. The innovations coexist with certain traditional values which either remain protected, as part of the cultural heritage, or are extensively reinterpreted to make them compatible with development values, as in the case of neo-Confucianism, for example (see Note 6 above).

- Finally, the growing recognition of the importance of the role of culture in development should not allow it to be forgotten that, for most of the major players on the international stage, the economic and political dimensions of development are still decisive and that this point of view is unlikely to lose its importance in the foreseeable future. Thus, the question of the international economic and political context will determine the chances of promoting sustainable human development incorporating a cultural dimension.

- These are the parameters within which all the development agencies must operate and which enable the relative weight of their contribution and the limits of their action to be properly assessed *vis-à-vis* the other major participants, whether public institutions or actors in the private sector. It is all the more remarkable that, as we shall now see, this joint effort should already have achieved significant results.

PART ONE

Progress report:
from economic growth
to human development

Introduction

First formulated in very general terms during the 1960s, the importance of the principle of incorporating a cultural dimension in development has been recognized, as we have seen, since the mid-1970s. It has also been the subject of scientific research conducted by anthropologists, sociologists and even economists specializing in the problems of development. In the context of the international institutions, the expression was first used in 1975 at the Accra Intergovernmental Conference on Cultural Policies in Africa, organized jointly by UNESCO and the OAU.[1]

Since the early 1980s, the concept has been one of the main thrusts of the programme of UNESCO's Culture Sector. At the same time the attention given to the non-economic factors of development in the other institutions of the United Nations system has also increased. Thus greater consideration has been paid to the social and, in certain cases, cultural aspects of development and to the formulation of new concepts in this field, namely sustainable development and human development.

These initiatives fall within the broader context of the United Nations Development Strategy defined for the four decades beginning in 1960. The main elements of this strategy, devised in the 1970s to help the economies of the developing countries catch up more rapidly, now explicitly include observations and recommendations concerning the human aspects of development.

1. UNESCO, *Final Report* of the Intergovernmental Conference on Cultural Policies in Africa, Accra, 1975, Paris, UNESCO, 1975. (UNESCO doc. SHC/MD/29.)

The related endeavours of various intergovernmental organizations (notably the Commission of the European Communities), certain countries acting within a framework of bilateral co-operation (in particular Canada, France, Germany, the Scandinavian countries and the United States) and, finally, the big NGOs involved in development assistance must also be taken into account.

This part of the review is devoted to an assessment of the progress made during this period, and its purpose is to make it possible to capitalize on the results of the innovative experiments and scientific studies carried out so far and also to map out the broad outlines of the methodological and experimental programme proposed in Part Three.

CHAPTER 1

The institutions of the United Nations system

According to its Charter, one of the missions of the United Nations Organization is 'to achieve international co-operation in solving international problems of an economic, social, cultural, or humanitarian character . . .'.[1] Thus, from the outset, the United Nations has had the task of encouraging economic and social progress at the world level. Hence the growing interest taken by the whole of the system in the problems of unequal development in different parts of the world.

Within the framework of this general mandate, the United Nations has at its disposal a number of bodies that deal comprehensively with the problems of development: the Economic and Social Council and its subsidiary bodies; the Commission for Social Development; and the five Regional Economic Commissions (Africa, Asia and the Pacific, Europe, Latin America and the Caribbean, and Western Asia). In addition, there are standing groups of experts responsible for development planning. The United Nations Secretariat itself analyses world economic and social trends and problems and publishes studies on development.[2]

1. United Nations, *Charter of the United Nations, Preamble, Purposes and Principles,* New York, United Nations, 1945.
2. United Nations, *Basic Facts about the United Nations,* pp. 104–6, New York, United Nations, 1990.

Development strategies

THE UNITED NATIONS INTERNATIONAL
DEVELOPMENT STRATEGY

The United Nations General Assembly announced the first United Nations Development Decade in 1960. Because of the relative failure of this initiative and the difficulties experienced in its implementation, the United Nations adopted an International Development Strategy for the three successive decades of 1970, 1980 and 1990. The purpose of this document is to present a world plan of action for the institutions of the system and their efforts to promote development over the period concerned. The changes in the strategy over these three Decades clearly reflect the transition from a preoccupation with predominantly economic solutions for the problems of development to a view of the various aspects and consequences of underdevelopment coloured by social and human considerations.

Thus, as regards achieving the aims of the World Plan of Action, the International Strategy for the Seventies (Second Decade) basically assumed that the social objectives would be attained through accelerated economic growth.

The difficulties of implementing this plan led the General Assembly to adopt, in 1974, a Recommendation for the establishment of a New International Economic Order and, in 1975, the strategy for meeting basic needs drawn up by the International Labour Organization (ILO).

The Recommendation and the Action Programme for the establishment of a New International Economic Order, supplemented by a Charter of Economic Rights and Duties of States, were designed to make it possible 'to close the ever-widening gap between the developed and the developing countries' and to ensure 'for the present and future generations, in peace and justice, an ever-increasing pace of social and economic development'.[3]

On this basis, the General Assembly at its 1980 session, drawing attention to the emergence of problems such as hyperinflation, high levels of unemployment, monetary instability and, in some countries, the revival of protectionism, again stressed the urgency of

3. United Nations, *Declaration and Programme of Action on the Establishment of a New International Economic Order*, New York, United Nations, 1974.

accelerated economic development in the developing countries with a view to bringing world economic growth into balance and, by this means, ensuring world peace and stability. Accordingly, the Strategy for the Eighties (Third Decade) introduced not only new economic and financial measures but also, for the first time, measures relating to the environment, housing, disaster relief and social development, without however always making explicit reference to the cultural aspects of development.

It was not until the adoption of the Strategy for the Nineties (Fourth Decade) that a change of approach was to become apparent, with its inclusion of the protection of the various 'cultural entities' as the sole specifically cultural objective in its mandate.[4] Furthermore, the aims and objectives established by the document relate to the notion of sustainable development and human development: improvement of the human condition in the developing countries and closing of the gap between the rich countries and the poor; extended participation for all, men and women, in the political and economic life of the nation; movement towards political systems based on the general will and respect for human rights; the adaptation of development to meet social needs.

But the economic objectives are now formulated in human terms: encouragement of the private sector, in order to promote the spirit of enterprise and innovation; a gradual rather than abrupt transition from traditional agriculture to modern farming methods; stimulation of the unstructured sector of the economy and self-employment to solve the problems of joblessness and low incomes.

As for the utilization of human resources, the aim is no longer simply to satisfy the labour requirements of the economy but to give free rein to the creative potential of the individual, the factor determining the course of development. Similarly, each country should choose its own approach to the utilization of human resources and the creation of institutions, depending on its national priorities, its values, its traditions, its culture and its stage of development.

All in all, some movement towards taking interactions between culture and development into account may be noted in the fundamental objectives of the Strategy and, to some extent, in the

4. United Nations, *Resolutions and Decisions Adopted by the General Assembly during its Forty-Fifth Session,* Vol. I: *Resolutions 45/1990,* New York, United Nations, 1990.

problems identified in the Preamble (admittedly in connection with sustainable development), but none of the policies and measures recommended or the action priorities defined or the evaluation scheduled for the end of the Decade refers to the need to take the cultural dimensions of development fully into account as is proposed in Part Three of this study.

On the other hand, it should be noted that the Resolution on the right to development adopted by the United Nations General Assembly at its 47th session includes cultural rights as such among human rights, as well as economic, social and political rights.[5] It would no doubt be beneficial for the Strategy to turn more to this resolution for its inspiration in the Decades to come.

THE BASIC NEEDS STRATEGY OF THE INTERNATIONAL LABOUR ORGANIZATION

This trend was first set in motion by the International Labour Organization (ILO) and its presentation of a strategy for meeting basic needs in the context of the World Employment Conference in 1976, later to be taken up by the United Nations. Consideration for the human and even, in some respects, the cultural factors of development is much more to the fore in the strategy devised by the ILO. In particular, the document states that basic needs 'include two elements. First, they include certain minimum requirements of a family for private consumption . . . . Second, they include essential services provided by and for the community at large, such as . . . educational and cultural facilities.'

Furthermore, the concept of basic needs 'should be placed within a context of national independence, the dignity of individuals and peoples and their freedom to chart their destiny without hindrance'. Thus, even before the 1980s when the United Nations Strategy took a new turn, the ILO was already defining basic human needs in other than purely material terms.

---

5. United Nations, *Resolution 47/123, Right to Development*, New York, United Nations, 1993.

The specialized agencies: recent developments

THE WORK OF UNESCO

Of all the specialized agencies it is UNESCO that has devoted most attention to the cultural dimension of development. UNESCO has proclaimed, studied and tested, in experimental projects and specialized training sessions, the importance of the cultural factors and the cultural impact of development. Moreover, the Organization has engaged in a number of activities in co-operation with other Specialized Agencies of the United Nations (in particular, the World Bank, the Food and Agriculture Organization of the United Nations (FAO), the United Nations Children's Fund (UNICEF), the United Nations Industrial Development Organization (UNIDO), the World Health Organization (WHO) and the United Nations Fund for Population Activities (UNFPA)).

During the 1980s, on the basis of the conclusions of the Mexico City Conference on Cultural Policies, UNESCO pursued its vital exploration of this complex subject. In particular, it carried out studies and research with a view to establishing the general conditions for integrating culture into development and gave support to action-based research aimed at bringing out the dynamic role that cultural factors can play in local development projects.

Other studies and meetings of experts have dealt with the interactions between culture and various sectors of economic and social development, for example techno-industrial development. UNESCO[6]

6. B. Kossou, *La dimension culturelle du développement en vue d'intégrer les facteurs socioculturels dans le Plan d'action de Lagos* [The Cultural Dimension of Development, with a View to Integrating Sociocultural Factors into the Lagos Plan of Action], Paris, UNESCO, 1985. (UNESCO doc. FMR/CLT/CD/85/160); UNESCO, *L'élaboration d'un accord culturel cadre à l'intention des États membres de la Communauté économique des États de l'Afrique de l'Ouest* [Draft of an Outline Cultural Agreement for the Member States of the Economic Community of the West African States], Paris, UNESCO, 1985. (UNESCO doc. FMR/CLT/CD/85/136); UDEAC/UNESCO, *La dimension culturelle du développement: recherche sur les pesanteurs socioculturelles comme blocage de réalisations économiques* [The Cultural Dimension of Development: Research into Sociocultural Inhibiting Factors Detracting from Economic Performance], Paris, UDEAC/UNESCO, 1986. (UNESCO doc. FMR/CC/CD/86/155.)

has in addition also investigated the incorporation of cultural aspects into certain economic and technical co-operation agreements (in particular, the Lomé Convention, the Lagos Plan of Action of the Organization of African Unity (OAU), the Economic Community of West African States (ECOWAS), and the Central African Customs and Economic Union (CACEU)). Finally, the Organization has taken numerous measures to promote training and raise cultural awareness among the economists and administrators responsible for development.[7]

In addition, UNESCO was the originator of two important initiatives linked with the problem of the cultural dimension of development, although their implementation involves joint action with the United Nations. First, there was the proclamation and implementation of the World Decade for Cultural Development, for which UNESCO is the lead organization. Then, more recently, came the establishment of a World Commission on Culture and Development set up by the United Nations General Assembly under the chairmanship of former United Nations Secretary-General Mr Xavier Pérez de Cuéllar, with UNESCO providing the executive secretariat.

The task of the commission is to prepare a report on the interactions between culture and development and on ways of solving the problems to which they give rise. At its twenty-sixth session, the General Conference of UNESCO also made the commission responsible for 'formulating proposals concerning urgent and long-term activities designed to meet cultural needs in the development context'. In short, the commission is asked to make recommenda-

---

7. D. Desjeux, *Essay on Training in Culture*, Paris, UNESCO, 1989. (UNESCO doc. CC/CSP/CP/22); UNESCO, Centre for Cultural Resources and Training, *Draft Training Programme for High-level Decision-makers in the Cultural Dimensions of their Tasks*, Paris, UNESCO, 1990. (UNESCO doc. CC/CSP/CP/03); L. Balmond, *Séminaire de sensibilisation des responsables d'agences d'intégration économique sur la dimension culturelle du développement* [Seminar to Alert Officials in Charge of Economic Integration Agencies to the Cultural Dimensions of Development], Paris, UNESCO, 1990. (UNESCO doc. CLT/90/WS/11); Thai National Commission for UNESCO, *Subregional Meeting on the Cultural Dimension of Development in South-East Asia, Bangkok, 2–5 July 1990*, Paris, UNESCO, 1991. (UNESCO doc. CLT/DEC/CP/010.)

tions for short- and long-term action for the purpose of clarifying policy formulation in the field of development and that of culture at national, regional and international levels. The paths along which the commission will need to work are as follows: interrelations between culture and development; cultural development; development, culture, population, environment and management; development, culture, education, science and technology, and economics; development and culture of democracy, ethics, human rights and peace; culture, development, the society of communication and cultural industries; cultural exchange, intercultural relations and development.

This report will be submitted to the General Conference of UNESCO and the United Nations General Assembly in 1995. The work of the commission may also be used to provide the basis of an agenda for culture and development to supplement the Brundtland Report and Agenda 21 adopted by the Rio World Conference on the Environment.

For the Decade and the commission the problems posed by interaction between culture and development play a key role. This is a more technical task since, in addition to the identification of the points of interaction, it implies the seeking out of approaches, methods and instruments – the subject of the present document – the aim of which is to introduce a cultural approach into the frameworks and instruments used for preparing, implementing and assessing development programmes, plans and projects.

THE WORK OF THE OTHER AGENCIES

Among the institutions and agencies of the United Nations, some, for example the United Nations Development Programme (UNDP), the United Nations Environment Programme (UNEP), the United Nations Centre for Human Settlements (UNCHS), WHO and UNFPA, have from the outset had a role explicitly associated with the problems of the human dimension of development. The United Nations University (UNU) and the United Nations Research Institute for Social Development (UNRISD), for their part, are conducting studies and research on the social and cultural dimensions of integrated development.

Since 1980, there has been a general trend throughout the United Nations system towards greater insistence on the non-economic aspects of development. A number of agencies have done research and undertaken projects bearing explicitly on the social, human and even cultural aspects of development. Though it makes no claim to be exhaustive, the following account attempts to show the scope and results of these experiments.

Within the general context of these activities, the 1980s and 1990s have been marked by two important contributions to the study of the humanization of development:

- the report of the Brundtland Commission (1987);
- the UNDP World Report published annually since 1990.

THE BRUNDTLAND REPORT: *OUR COMMON FUTURE*

In 1987, at the 42nd session of the United Nations General Assembly, the World Commission on the Environment and Development, mandated by the United Nations and presided over by Mrs G. H. Brundtland, Prime Minister of Norway, submitted a report entitled *Our Common Future,* which introduced the novel concept of 'sustainable development' which takes into account the conditions of the natural and human environment in developmental activities.

According to the terms of the report, 'sustainable development' meets the needs of the present without compromising the ability of subsequent generations to meet the needs of the future.

The concept of sustainable development implies a global approach and a long-term strategy which, while giving priority to environmental problems, also deals at world level with the problems of population and human resources, food supply, energy, industry and urban development.

However, when it comes to describing the conditions, other than purely economic, technical and institutional, for identifying the needs of the present and ensuring popular participation in development and the balanced management of the natural and human ecosystems, the Brundtland Report restricts itself to recommending changes in human attitudes. These tasks could, indeed, only be successfully carried out in the context of behaviour and values rooted in the cultures governing the relations between populations and the general environment and nature. In other words, the report does not address the question of the cultural 'sustainability' of development, which involves taking cultural factors into account and recognizing the cultural values that promote development.

THE UNDP HUMAN DEVELOPMENT REPORT

Beginning in 1990, UNDP decided to produce an annual report on the human dimension of development whose more global approach to the analysis of development is a considerable step forward. The Foreword to the first report, for example, states that 'while growth in national production (GNP) is absolutely necessary to meet all essential human objectives, what is important is to study how this growth translates – or fails to translate – into human development in various societies'. The point is that some have achieved 'a high level of human development despite a low per capita income' whereas others have failed to translate 'their comparatively high income-levels and rapid economic growth into commensurate levels of human development'. The description of the aims of the *Human Development Report* clearly opens the door to a cultural approach to development, but its various chapters tend to treat development in social rather than cultural terms.

Thus, the concept of human development is defined by means of a series of indicators which enable all the human and social data to be compared by country. However, as regards the developing countries, these indicators relate essentially to living conditions. By contrast, where the industrialized countries are concerned, some of the indicators relate to ways of life, in particular under the headings of 'human distress' and 'weakening social fabric'. Other indicators implicitly refer to problems of a cultural nature, such as differences in the treatment of men and women, health, education and training, wealth and poverty, and urban overpopulation, as we shall see in Part Two of this study.

In short, the human development characteristic of certain developing countries is not reflected in the indicators proposed – with one exception. In its 1992 report, in addition to other indicator tables, UNDP includes a section devoted to political freedom indicators: personal security, rule of law, freedom of expression, political participation and equality of opportunity. But, in UNDP's human development indicators, the question of cultural values and cultural factors and effects goes largely ignored. As for the question of mentalities, modes of thought, lifestyles and role models or the question of the material culture, i.e. the economy (the production, trade and consumption models that exist in all societies), these are not yet shown in the report.

The 1993 report focuses on the notion of participation, whose cultural significance need not be stressed. The authors of the report draw two principal conclusions: firstly that, by reason of its principle, the logic of the market guarantees of itself the free participation of all in economic life, and secondly that participation is the privileged expression of democracy in action. In opposition to these two main rules are state control of the market and the substitution of the nation-state for society and still more the individual. But the report finds that the market should be more 'people-friendly'. Participation is also a matter of access to employment, which the pure logic of the market does not necessarily guarantee for all. What is more, it postulates governmental decentralization, regionalization of power and consultation with the population as forms of democracy. Democracy is the fruit of a medium- or long-term learning process. Howevef this may be, it is an essential condition for the survival of societies and, more generally, of development.

Thus the 1993 report is a big step forward in the quest for bases and conditions for truly human development but, as it points out in an annex (Annex 2), the gap between the notion of human development and the production of appropriate numerical indicators is still very wide. The latter could relate primarily to longevity, levels of education and possible access to resources. They would measure a minimum above which other dimensions of personal development might be addressed. Apart from a short passage on 'social and cultural' development, the question of the cultural dimension of development as such is not so far addressed.

Innovative experiments

Apart from the change of tack reflected in the broad strategic documents mentioned above, many institutions have prepared studies or carried out projects which take the cultural factors clearly into account using methods they have worked out themselves to meet their own needs. At this point, a brief reference to a few significant examples could well be useful.

THE WORLD BANK

Since the early 1980s, the World Bank has been experimenting with a number of techniques designed to take into account either the needs of the populations affected by development projects or their cultural values and practices, which in some cases could play a dynamic role.

For the purpose the Bank introduced a new method for evaluating some of its projects, the results of these being assessed by the target population themselves. The Bank also had case-studies produced on the role of sociological variables in rural development.

In 1982, the Bank tried out the 'beneficiary assessment' technique with a view to improving the design and implementation of its projects. This technique has brought to the fore several factors that are fundamental to the success of development projects. Thus, it is often necessary to improve communications between beneficiaries and project staff, with particular attention to living conditions, social stratification and the perceived needs of the groups concerned. Finally, there can be no doubt that participation by the community is vital if a project is to succeed.

The object of beneficiary assessment is to understand a project from the point of view of its intended beneficiaries, in the belief that if the project is planned and implemented with the knowledge of people's values, responsive to their needs and adapted to their behaviour, it is more likely to be successfully implemented and lead the way to sustained development.

The underlying assumption of this approach is that planners and managers of development projects do not normally have a deep enough understanding of the world they are trying to change, nor can this be expected. This understanding is found primarily among those who inhabit that world. To gain this understanding, planners and managers need to seek assistance from third parties who can simultaneously understand the goals of the project and know the values and perceptions of its intended beneficiaries. As such, beneficiary assessment provides one avenue among many which may bring the human, cultural dimension more fully into what is still the insufficiently concrete field of development.

However, it seems that the ascendancy of the purely economic approach has been an obstacle to the general adoption of this technique, as has the difficulty of recruiting competent local researchers capable of 'sufficient empathy to inspire confidence, while maintaining the right and necessary distance for objectivity'.

The World Bank has also had studies made of over sixty rural development projects to which it has lent its support, with a view to discovering what lessons could be learned from the use of sociocultural factors. A general report based on these studies[8] covers the various aspects of rural development: irrigation, creation of new agricultural establishments, stockfarming and grazing, small-scale fishing, forestry and reafforestation and rural road-building. Sociological lessons have been drawn from an assessment of the projects, the general message of which may be summed up in the need to have projects 'made to measure' for the population. 'Giving priority to people' means making the social organization of production systems the explicit concern of development policies and programmes and constructing development projects around the types of production, cultural models, needs and aptitudes of the populations living in the area of the project.

For example, the role of sociocultural factors in the development of road networks in the rural environment is studied so as to bring out its impact on the social, cultural and economic life of the communities concerned and to assess its desired (or undesirable) effects, highlighting those on such areas as access to markets and services, job opportunities, the emergence of a regional structuring of rural development and, in some cases, imbalance in the amelioration of living conditions for different communities, the growth of a migratory movement towards the town, changes in women's situation, receptivity to innovation and so forth.

These studies have shown on the whole that taking into account the problems of sociocultural compatibility between the agronomic logic of the projects and local agrarian practices had a positive economic impact, since projects which took these problems into account in the preliminary planning stage produced results that were twice as good as those that did not. Moreover, it transpired that those in charge of the successful projects had not sought out innovation for its own sake but rather had tended to incorporate local cultural practices and use local social structures in the implementation stage of the projects.

---

8. M. Cernea, *Putting People First: Sociological Variables in Rural Development*, Washington, D.C., World Bank/Oxford University Press, 1985.

The Culture of Maintenance project is an interinstitutional initiative (World Bank, UNESCO, UNIDO). The aim is to study the
factors contributing to the shortcomings in the maintenance of
infrastructure and equipment in Africa and the local population's
poorly developed sense of responsibility for public property. This
situation appears to be the result of ignorance of new technologies
and a communications gap between the relevant decision-making
structures and users.

It would therefore be useful to revive or instil a 'culture of
maintenance' in these populations and to introduce appropriate
incentive systems. The project calls for a series of case-studies. An
investigation of the traditional maintenance systems and current
problems would make it possible to analyse the link between the
population and its heritage and to establish the nature and strength
of the sense of ownership with respect to certain types of collective
property. The importance of the origin (whether foreign or not) of
the goods would also be analysed.

UNICEF

Already in 1986, UNICEF, assessing the results of development
projects initiated by national authorities or bilateral or multilateral
co-operation organizations, concluded that, in these projects, cultural factors, in particular ways of life and value systems, had been
largely overlooked.[9] This explains the setbacks encountered by
many of these operations, which failed to mobilize the populations
concerned.

'It is therefore vital', concluded the report, 'to model development projects closely on local cultural and material possibilities and
difficulties.' Thus, the report proclaimed the need to promote a new
conception of development, based on the adaptability of strategies,
projects and executants to the different needs of each society, as
reflected in its culture, whether rural, urban or suburban.

At the same time, UNICEF organized numerous experiments in
Africa involving grass-roots participation in development programmes. The aim of these experiments, particularly those in

9. *UNICEF, A portée de la main: l'avenir des enfants d'Afrique* [Within
   Arm's Reach: the Future of the Children of Africa], New York,
   UNICEF, 1986.

Burkina Faso and Mali, was 'to encourage communities to analyse their own needs' and 'to seek solutions to the fundamental problems of daily life' by calling upon 'both mutual assistance and the co-operation of governmental, national and local bodies', the aim being to improve the well-being of the children by transferring responsibility to the communities themselves. The participation of the population concerned extends to the economic management of health activities.

In Niger, an integrated programme involving areas as different as health, education, female illiteracy and environmental protection was launched. These programmes are supplemented by the provision of training for local project officials, which enables them to take charge of their own development.

In short, all these initiatives are based on two principles: the proximity of assistance with respect to the beneficiary communities and the involvement of the latter in the identification, practical economic implementation and even monitoring and assessment of the projects. UNICEF's activities in this field are broken down into 'zonal programmes'.

THE WORLD HEALTH ORGANIZATION (WHO)

WHO's mandate, expressed in the most general terms, is to 'raise all peoples to the highest possible level of health'. To that end a global strategy was formulated consisting of eight essential elements. Of these, education on health problems, the welfare of mother and child, including family planning, and the prevention and control of major epidemics have an obvious cultural dimension that is given particular consideration in the special programme and world strategy for the prevention and control of AIDS, in which information and education play a paramount role. UNESCO and WHO have set up for this purpose a joint in-school education programme which the two organizations are planning to extend to extra-school education, given the risks run by peoples of all categories and geographical origins.

The role of education in the prevention of AIDS is firstly to impart information relevant to the sociocultural context and secondly to awaken public responsibility and thus bring about changes in attitudes and behaviour towards the disease and the social phenomenon it represents.

The cultural aspects of the problem, which are fairly obvious, first concern the approach to be taken by educators and the providers of information *vis-à-vis* the different publics concerned: infants/young people/adults, men/women, urban/rural populations anchored in traditional cultures or living in a modern socio-economic environment. Informers and educators first need to question themselves about their own culture, habits and behaviour towards the disease and sexuality. As for the populations concerned, their attitude may be conditioned by their own value systems and spiritual or religious references, whence the possibility of reluctance on their part to address the question in practical terms. The educational materials will therefore firstly concern the preparation of the teachers for their task and the teaching techniques to be used when dealing with subjects that are taboo or at least intimate – things that are generally left unspoken. Putting such a programme into effect inevitably conflicts with ways of thought, life and behaviours and attitudes in the field of sexuality. One of the major difficulties also lies in the great diversity of language and religious practice among the target populations and school enrolment rates of young and older children, the latter category being regarded as particularly vulnerable. For significant results to be achieved in this field, therefore, a continuous effort is required to improve both the cultural and technical content of the information media used and the training of educators.

UNITED NATIONS FUND FOR POPULATION ACTIVITIES (UNFPA)

Established in its present form in 1987, UNFPA today is the leading international source of assistance for developing countries' demographic programmes, mostly family-planning projects.

The role of the Fund is to help governments formulate their population and family policy objectives and programmes, to enhance the understanding of the role of demographic factors (increase in population, fertility, mortality, geographical distribution and migrations of population). The Fund works in these fields by developing education, communication, training, research and policy-making activities, and it also runs special programmes for women, young people, and the old and disabled.

In all these activities UNFPA has found it necessary to pay more and more attention to the way in which sociocultural factors affect attitudes in the population area and their implications for the formulation and implementation of demographic policies and programmes. To this end, a joint programme has been worked out between UNFPA and UNESCO (the latter being responsible for its implementation) in which the accent will be on changes in fertility (or birth rate) and migration from country to town or to other parts of the world. It will also aim at drawing up an overall picture of the demographic situation in the various countries in order to make suggestions on policy-making.

THE UNITED NATIONS FOOD AND AGRICULTURE ORGANIZATION (FAO)

For several years FAO has been taking the cultural context into consideration in its rural development projects. In this connection, its planned joint project with UNESCO's International Fund for the Promotion of Culture (IFPC) deserves mention. Entitled 'Forest and Culture in Asia',[10] this project is aimed at maintaining the forest resources of South Asia and the traditional knowledge, know-how, skills and spiritual values of the peoples who derive their livelihood from them but at the same time consider that certain trees are sacred and that cutting them down is forbidden.

In operational terms, the project involves enabling the local population to co-manage forest resources with the officials of the forestry services, thus making use of their knowledge, values, modes of expression and territorial rights, in combination with modern forms of silviculture. Accordingly, the decision-makers will have to be made aware of the value of the sociocultural factors and of their incorporation into the training and management programmes of the Specialized Agencies. Finally, these factors will have to be taken into account in the policies and legislative measures adopted. The countries involved in the project are India, Indonesia, Malaysia, Nepal, Thailand and Viet Nam.

10. UNESCO/FAO, *Forest and Culture in Asia,* Bangkok, UNESCO/FAO, 1992.

THE UNITED NATIONS DEVELOPMENT PROGRAMME (UNDP)

As the biggest world-level mechanism for multilateral technical co-operation and pre-investment, UNDP conducts its development-promoting activities by means of country, world and interregional programmes and has brought out the previously mentioned *Human Development Report* every year since 1990.

Active in over 150 countries and territories, the organization coordinates about 5,900 development projects in numerous economic and social sectors under plurinational, regional and national programmes. The total value of the projects is US$7,500 million, 80 per cent of which goes to the least-developed countries within the framework of their national programmes. UNDP assistance is incorporated in the overall national or regional plans. For the planning period 1992–96, the emphasis is on the national level of implementation. The themes for the same period are poverty and development.

As we have already seen, UNDP pays increasing attention, in the descriptive part of its report on human development, to non-economic factors of development, and this concern is beginning to be reflected in the principal policies behind its action.

The general thrust of the annual report made by the UNDP Administrator of the Council of Governors at the 1993 session, for example, largely takes its cue from the main principles of human development.[11]

This report states that 'in the new development paradigm, economic growth is still important but increasingly conditioned by experimentation on its positive impact on the welfare of individuals and societies'. Beneficiaries' involvement at all stages of development is regarded as essential. Conversely, discrimination, particularly with regard to women, becomes an obstacle that is not merely unacceptable but also grave in its consequences. Democracy and respect for human rights are likewise absolutely necessary in development processes.

In the same report, an assessment of experiments conducted in countries at three levels of development and in different continents

11. UNDP, *1991 and 1992 Reports by the Administrator to the UNDP Governing Council*, New York, UNDP, 1993.

points to three important conclusions: development is both political and multisectoral (sectoral projects rarely have a decisive impact); development has to have its roots at the national level and be people-based, provided those people feel that development belongs to them and that they are capable of planning it and putting it into effect; and national development has to be moved to the world level and to an international environment in which it can be feasible. In short, development is increasingly seen in terms of the improvement of the human condition and going beyond economic growth as such.

This change, slow as it has been, began to be noted in the 1980s in the projects and programmes designed and carried out by UNDP on its own or in co-operation with other institutions with responsibilities in the fields concerned. This is how UNDP came to take non-economic factors into account and forged methodological tools for the purpose, in particular for project or programme assessment.[12]

In addition, in certain projects contact is made with the people concerned in the form of direct help where this is needed; in other words, putting such projects into effect may require local participation in certain activities.

In other types of project, support for 'institutional reinforcement' at the request of the authorities consists in creating new or improving existing structures, for example, teacher-training centres in the case of education.

As regards methodological instruments, UNDP has brought out project evaluation guides for assessors in which there is a 'relevance' heading which asks the following questions: Is the purpose of the project still valid and relevant? Can proofs of this be given? Another heading relates to the way in which the concerns of the beneficiaries are reflected in the projects and their needs met. The half-way assessment may call for a change of direction in the project. The final evaluation should give recommendations on project follow-up on the basis of a report on effects on beneficiaries.

---

12. UNDP, *Guidelines for Evaluators*, New York, UNDP, 1991; UNESCO, *UNDP Policies, Procedures and Guidelines for Project and Programme Evaluation*, Paris, UNESCO, 1993. (UNESCO doc. BPE.93/WS/1); UNESCO, *Operational Project Evaluation*, Paris, UNESCO, 1992. (UNESCO doc. CEU/Inf. Series/9–Rev.)

In addition, UNDP has had an ongoing checklist produced of proposed projects. The list is in the form of a questionnaire with the following headings: context of the project, justification (including potential beneficiaries), objectives (general and immediate), products, activities, inputs (needs met), risks, antecedents, legal context, budget, timetable, feasibility and durability of the project.

Relevant though these prior evaluation or analysis tables may be, they are still partly based on the notion of technical feasibility, availability of human resources and meeting the needs of the target populations, and in this way are limited to an internal interrogation of the project or its immediate human and institutional environment. Moreover, the exclusively rationalistic logic of the project and its means of implementation continue to predominate. In addition, it is still difficult to understand what has presided over its conception and how it is placed in relation to the target populations: their lifestyles, value systems, knowledge and know-how are not considered as a major criterion for the success or failure of the project. It should therefore be possible for tables for the prior evaluation or analysis of projects to take second place to such important realities as cultural diversity and the existence of economic, political or social attitudes specific to the populations concerned.

As for projects by country, these are very unequal in their reflection of UNDP's basic options, especially as regards the notion of human development. Here are two contrasting examples:
1. A consultative note concerning Benin aimed at enlisting the co-operation of the Specialized Agencies in the drafting of a five-year programme (1993–97) based on the priorities laid down by a decision of UNDP's Governing Council taken at its thirty-seventh session (1990). Among these priorities, grass-roots participation, environmental protection, the integration of women in the development process and the promotion of the private sector may be regarded as having something to do with taking the cultural dimension into account. The strategy proposed is one of sustainable economic development and, on the social side, action to combat poverty. In administrative terms, there are recommendations to encourage the decentralization and deconcentration of administration, with a view to strengthening participation, especially where women and the rural population are concerned. The main thrust of the programme is to take human development into account as a frame of reference for all

the activities of the fifth programming cycle.

2. The other illustration is the UNDP evaluation report on the Central African Republic in so far as it contains a number of general observations on the local cultural and social situation: diversity of ethnic groups and languages with a single language of communication, weakness of the productive sector aggravated by inefficient practices (itinerant agriculture on burnt-off land, animal husbandry 'on the move', mining 'bordering on the informal', low level of monetarization of the economy). Observations of this type could be used as benchmarks for project assessment and monitoring.

It may therefore be said that the 'new deal' in development, as it appears to UNDP, is reflected more at the level of general documents than in projects and programmes. But the situation is changing radically and no definitive judgement is possible for the moment.

THE REGIONAL ECONOMIC COMMISSIONS

The five Regional Economic Commissions, subsidiary bodies of the United Nations Economic and Social Council,[13] have already engaged in some activities – and others are in preparation – linked with the specific problems of social development, and are taking the 'cultural variable' into account.

These activities include studies or projects relating to the role of women in development in Western Asia (Arab States), a training workshop on cultural conditions and the role of women in the application and development of science and technology in Africa, a conference on the major economic and social trends and prospects in Europe and consideration of the environmental impact of government policies, plans and programmes in every field.

The United Nations Regional Economic Commission in the Asia–Pacific Region has done much work and held many meetings on the social and human aspects of development and the environment, including the formulation of appropriate indicators. For its part, the Economic Commission for Latin America and the Caribbean has carried out a study of the cultural dimensions of a creative

13. United Nations, *Basic Facts about the United Nations,* op. cit., p. 12.

and balanced economic and social transformation in which the internationalization of culture would result in an 'intercultural tissue' that would give to modernity all the force it needs, provided that it is linked to a renewed sense of civic awareness.

Finally, in connection with the mid-term review of the World Decade for Cultural Development, the United Nations General Assembly at its 46th session invited the United Nations Secretary-General and the Director-General of UNESCO to arrange for the regional economic commissions to evaluate the cultural factors influencing development as a potential creator of jobs and generator of income.[14]

---

14. United Nations, *Resolution A/46/157, World Decade for Cultural Development,* operative part, paragraph 3(a), New York, United Nations, 1991.

CHAPTER 2

The experience of other co-operation agencies and the action of non-governmental organizations

Multilateral co-operation

It should first be noted that, under the Maastricht Treaty on European Union, the Commission of the European Communities (CEC) has power to deal with cultural affairs. Thus, the Treaty states that 'The Community shall take cultural aspects into account in its action under other provisions of this Treaty' (education, vocational training, youth, public health, consumer protection, transport and telecommunications, research and technological development, environment, and development co-operation), in addition to exercising its previous powers in the economic sphere, assigned to it by the Treaty of Rome.[1]

THE LOMÉ CONVENTION

The Lomé Convention, administered by Directorate-General VIII of the Commission, governs development co-operation between the Community and the signatory states of Africa, the Caribbean and the Pacific (the ACP States). There is explicit reference to the role of the cultural and social dimension in the development of the sig-' natory states in Title XI, Chapter 1 of the revised Convention, which states that 'The design, appraisal, execution and evaluation of

---

1. *Maastricht Treaty*, Title IX, Article 128.

each project or programme shall be based on understanding of, and regard for, the cultural and social features of the milieu.' This involves in particular:

assessment of opportunities for participation by the population, thorough knowledge of the milieu and eco-systems concerned, study of local technology and of other appropriate forms of technology, provision of relevant information for all those concerned in the design and execution of operations, including technical co-operation personnel, evaluation of the human resources available for executing and maintaining projects, provision of integrated programmes for the promotion of human resources.

The chapter goes on to state that:

The following shall be taken into account in the appraisal of all projects and programmes:
(a) under the heading of cultural aspects: adaptation to the cultural milieu and the implications for that milieu, integration and enhancement of the local cultural heritage, notably value systems, way of life, modes of thought and know-how, materials and styles, methods of information acquisition and transmission, interaction between man and his environment and between the people and natural resources;
(b) under the heading of social aspects, the impact of such projects or programmes as regards the reinforcement of capacities and structures for self-development, improvement of the status and role of women, the involvement of young people in economic, cultural and social development, contribution to the satisfaction of the population's basic cultural and physical needs, the promotion of employment and training, the balance between demographic structure and other resources, social and interpersonal relationships, structures, methods and forms of production and processing.[2]

LIST OF CRITERIA

The CEC finances many assistance projects for developing countries, notably within the framework of the Lomé Convention. In the light of its experience with that Convention, the Commission has drawn up a list of cultural factors, with a view to adapting the assis-

2.   *Lomé IV Convention*, Part XI, Chap. I, Articles 142 and 143.

tance to the special requirements of the different geographical and cultural areas of the Convention's beneficiary countries.[3]

This list covers the following four groups of factors:

Social organization of the population concerned

- Structure (ethnic, political, age-groups, religious, linguistic, etc.).
- Status of and relations between groups, hierarchies (by age, sex, lineage, possessions, etc.).
- Decision-making process and power within the group and with regard to the outside world.
- Demography (fertility, life expectancy, foreseeable trend) and mobility (patterns of movement, direction, duration). In the case of migration: extent, reasons, origin, destination, duration, sex and age of migrants, consequences for the area of origin, methods of movement, cost.
- Situation regarding basic needs (nutrition, water, health and hygiene, housing).
- Employment (type, levels, conditions).
- Criteria for values and social prestige.

Family organization

- Family size and structure (for various representative groups).
- Interpersonal relations, links with regard to authority/subordination, sharing of responsibility in the family (e.g. budgeting, decision-making, etc.).
- Who is the head of the family?
- Allocation of tasks within the family.
- Specific position and role of women.

Economic organization

- Forms of ownership, devolution, transmission and inheritance of land, equipment, etc.
- Role of money, relationship between wealth and social value.
- Activity (agriculture, livestock farming, crafts, commerce, transport, looking after children and the family, etc.) and productive workers (specify: crops, food crops – cash crops/own consumption, other crops, other activities): specify men/women/children, if not done under 'Family organization' above.

3. CEC, *Commission of the European Communities: Compendium of Instructions and Directives concerning Cultural Co-operation*, Brussels, CEC, 1990.

- Principal products and methods of production.
- Organization of work, calendar giving workload at principal seasons of year. If wage-earning, specify working and living conditions, pay and origin of wage-earners.
- Instruments and tools, equipment, technologies.
- Trade, transport and processing of products.
- Prices at different stages.
- Incomes (cash/kind), indebtedness and savings – credit: conditions governing access and repayment, repayment percentage found.
- Propensity to consume, invest, innovate (distribution and use of income, e.g. purchase of sheet metal, bicycles, millet beer, etc.).
- Access to agricultural extension services and to the results of scientific and technical research.

Cultural factors
- General or vocational knowledge (specify type and since when acquired, training structures), in particular: literacy rate, ability to monitor accounts, keep the books of a co-operative, etc.).
- Beliefs, customs, value systems.
- Taboos (in relation to food, natural resources, interpersonal relations, etc.).
- Attitudes towards modernization, attachment to traditional wisdom.
- Characteristic behaviour patterns (e.g. use of leisure time, hospitality, aspirations).
- Relations with authorities (central/regional) and institutions.
- Self-help efforts: collegiate bodies (e.g. village committees), collective work, etc., and scope in this field, in particular process of innovation: initiative (individual or collective, private or public), obstacles (such as social inequality) and dissemination (process of imitation, persuasion, etc.).
- People's interest in the project (if they have been consulted), and/or in earlier projects (are they maintaining/operating?, etc.).

Though highly elaborate and complete, this list does not arrange the factors in question in any particular hierarchical order, so that the structuralizing nature of some of them is not immediately apparent. Moreover, 'the Commission is aware that this grid is no more than a guide and source of inspiration. It could subsequently be improved, in particular by taking into account the major cultural differences by geographic area.'

The Commission of the European Communities' 'Evaluation' unit has also produced a project cycle management manual, with the aid of the departments responsible for Community assistance and other experts from the Member States or the governments of the ACP (Asia, Caribbean, Pacific) countries which are states parties to the Lomé Convention. The manual points out that one of the reasons for the failure of projects is the absence of the necessary 'respect for the socio-cultural values of the principal players' and that, 'among the factors ensuring the viability of a project, the socio-cultural aspects should appear in the documents drawn up for this purpose' (CEC, Methods and Instruments for Project Cycle Management Series, February 1993).

THE ORGANISATION FOR ECONOMIC CO-OPERATION AND DEVELOPMENT

The purpose of the Organisation for Economic Co-operation and Development (OECD), founded in 1961, is to promote policies designed to encourage economic growth and therefore stable employment, to develop world trade, to promote economic and social well-being in its member countries and to contribute to healthy and harmonious development of the world economy, including the stimulation and co-ordination of member countries' action to help the developing countries.

Among the statutory objectives of the OECD, promoting economic and social well-being and harmonizing efforts to help the developing countries naturally have cultural implications.

A Development Centre set up within the Organisation plans and carries out research programmes, particularly on macroeconomic policies for both the short term (economic stabilization policies) and the medium and long term (sustainable growth and development policies). In this general framework it is interesting, from our viewpoint, to assess the cultural dimension of structural adjustment policies.

The studies that have been done relate, among other things, to decision-makers' attitudes towards the future, those attitudes being dependent on their mind-set. They also bring out the role of socio-cultural antagonisms in the difficulty of making economic policy decisions. They then look at national decision-makers' attitudes to co-operation for development and specifically at the way in which these problems are approached and handled. For this purpose the OECD Development Centre has constructed a model in which the various components of global policy can be used in various combinations to meet the diversity of the situations to be dealt with, with particular regard to different societies' socio-economic choices.

Lastly, an analysis of situations in the field is designed to enable the areas in which techniques and methods of dealing with problems are the same, regardless of the sociocultural context considered, to be distinguished from those where the specific nature of mental attitudes, cultures, religions and family structures is unlikely to evolve otherwise than in obedience to its own dynamic.

The 'variable geometry' models constructed by OECD make it possible for the big development assistance organizations to go some way to meeting the need for major social/cultural diversities, perceived at nation-state level, to be taken into account. Conversely, the dualism between the introduction of new technologies and organizational processes and the retention of local cultures raises the question of the interactions which will inevitably arise between these two sets of activities, mentalities and cultures.

Bilateral co-operation

THE CANADIAN INTERNATIONAL DEVELOPMENT AGENCY

As indicated in a briefing document issued by the Canadian International Development Agency (CIDA), 'Canadian co-operation is being directed more and more towards aid transfer strategies which make best use of the participation of the poorest populations in their own development'. The approaches and methods employed in social and community development can help to redirect aid and 'to implement anti-poverty programmes and projects in a more appropriate manner, by taking the social dimensions (respect for local resources, values and pace of change) into account in accordance with a self-development approach by the population'.

From the outset, CIDA has been concerned about social and community development. However, Canadian co-operation is now tending increasingly towards strategies designed no longer to assist the developing countries but to make best use of the participation of the poorest populations in their own development.

To this end, more and more use is being made of the approaches and methods of social and community development in general to redirect aid and find ways and means of making it effective. From now on, in whatever action they take to improve living conditions in the developing countries, the Canadian partners will always have to bear in mind the respect there has to be for local human and natural resources and the values and potential rates of change which local populations are so concerned to hold on to.

Accordingly, the agency has recently set up a transsectoral section for the social dimensions of development with a view to inviting the technical sectors to take into account the social dimensions of their projects – that is, the analysis, by sociologists and anthropologists, of the present and foreseeable behaviour of the groups involved in economic growth and technological innovation strategies. With regard to the new projects supported by the agency, the work of the social and community development sector will be directed along the following main lines: knowledge of the milieu, participation of the population, respect for personal rights, social development and strengthening of the institutional framework. The managers of CIDA's projects will therefore have to lay the stress on four preliminary conditions: identification of the target groups, encouragement of local participation, measurement of the social impact of every action, and development of national institutions capable of taking over from outside partners.

UNITED STATES AGENCY FOR INTERNATIONAL DEVELOPMENT

In 1975 the United States Agency for International Development (USAID) began using a new method of evaluating projects it was considering supporting. In its original form, this method, called 'social soundness analysis' and drawn up at the request of Congress in order to formulate new guidelines and standards to be applied to projects supported by USAID, was to serve as a means of assessing the compatibility of the project proposed with the potential beneficiaries' own sociocultural context, to increase the potential for the project benefits to spread and for an equitable distribution of project benefits and burdens among the affected groups. Towards the end of the 1970s, the agency was employing over fifty full-time anthropologists and other social analysts on this programme. Broader acceptance of using social–cultural analyses in project design was facilitated because of the large number of USAID personnel that had worked at the village level in developing countries.

The above method no doubt clashed with certain of USAID's administrative practices and the classic bias towards purely economic and quantitative analysis. However, since the beginning of the 1980s, USAID has modified its policy, with development projects increasingly replaced by economic programmes intended to encourage political reforms at central government level and based on the free play of market forces and scientific and technological progress.

According to an evaluation undertaken in 1990 of the effects of the use of social soundness analysis, there has been wide recognition of the value of this approach, but inadequate organizational learning from its use. The analyses of economists and technicians continue to appear more credible and many social scientists reportedly have not been willing to challenge the basic goals, assumptions and logic of proposed projects. Finally, institutional structures and procedures tend to work against the systematic use of sociocultural analysis, which some administrative decision-makers regard as making their task more complicated and laborious.

However, social soundness analysis was considered most helpful by project directors when used throughout the project cycle and combined with cost–benefit analysis and studies of household choices and of factors affecting consumption and saving. It was therefore decided that it would henceforth be concentrated particularly on the following: participants and beneficiaries, sociocultural feasibility, institutions and organizations, politics, decision-making and national, regional and local linkages, indicators and impact, sustainability and key assumptions regarding the nature of the problem and the proposed solutions.

MINISTRY OF CO-OPERATION (FRANCE)

It was its recognition of the stagnation in rural productivity throughout Africa south of the Sahara and the comparison between that situation and the population figures in the countries concerned (70 per cent of the total population of this subregion) that prompted the

French Ministry of Co-operation to ask a group of experts from both research institutes and Franco-African co-operation organizations to carry out an in-depth study of the reasons for this situation and to formulate solutions based on the realities of life in Africa. Three goals were set:

1. To formulate and propose policies, principles, approaches and methods (not one single method) designed to solve the practical problems encountered on the ground.
2. To pursue this clarification work by supporting a number of meaningful actions with the African authorities concerned.
3. To organize the study of specific questions either by agro-ecological areas or by subject (irrigated perimeters, for example).

Four principles were laid down for future action at grass-roots level:

1. The variety of situations calls for differentiated forms of action and technical solutions.
2. Projects are only effective if local, regional and national levels are all linked together in carrying them out and if the short, medium and long terms are all borne in mind.
3. The strategies of all the different players concerned – rural population, governments, development structures, sponsors, NGOs and other economic operators – have to be integrated.
4. Projects have to be based on explicit compromises.

In conclusion, three key ideas should be borne in mind:

1. Simple solutions are ruled out because the situations are too complex and diverse.
2. The various players concerned, and first and foremost the farming population, with their culture, objectives and strategies, have to become full partners with whom every action has to be negotiated.
3. Each action has to be viewed at its level of relevance in terms of time and concrete economic, social and cultural conditions.

The culture of the players concerned has to be considered from several angles:

- the links between the cultural system, social structures and technological development;
- the influence of external cultures on rural cultures and those of African management grades;
- the taking into account and re-creation of certain cultural values related to the requirements of change.

The ministry has had a methodological guide produced on the

planning of local development which is intended for development workers or trainees in Africa, NGO officials and technical co-operation workers. This guide stresses the need to inform decision-makers in the groups and structures concerned with the local planning operation, ensuring that the people concerned make their own diagnosis and self-analysis and that they are given a detailed explanation of the conclusions reached by the specialists. This explanatory phase is designed to involve the communities concerned in the search for solutions and to have the proposals understood by the heads of the people's structures and outside partners. In conclusion, the guide points out that development at grass-roots level is a lengthy process which needs to be flexible and to be based on genuine in-depth self-analysis at that level. That would also be the moment to set out clearly the difficulties and constraints of the situation and possible ways of solving them. Lastly, it is not possible to promote local initiatives unless national rural development policy is liberal enough to allow some re-examination of existing command structures at rural level.

THE FINNISH INTERNATIONAL DEVELOPMENT AGENCY

The Finnish International Development Agency (FINNIDA), which comes under the Ministry for Foreign Affairs, has carried out a number of development projects in which cultural factors have been taken into account, using a method associating the agency itself, as the sponsor, Finnish consultancies specializing in the fields concerned and the Institute for Development Studies of the University of Helsinki, which works in collaboration with the local universities of the beneficiary countries.

The purpose of a water supply and drainage project in Sri Lanka, for example, was not only to carry out operations for the development of water resources and to improve local sanitation conditions but also to produce social, economic and management studies of use to the project.[4]

When it was over, the project's initiators and team of observers came to the following conclusions:

4.   CEC, op. cit.

- the sociocultural components need to be integrated not only in the planning of technological projects but also in activities in progress. In addition, projects' sociocultural impact needs to be studied when they are completed;
- in the study related to the project, the sociocultural components were roughly classified in the following way: socio-economic context, cognitive dimensions of culture, technology and intercultural contact.

For the authors of the project, socio-economic information was important for identifying the target groups to which the development projects best lent themselves, laying the foundations for planning and identifying the obstacles to development.

The cognitive dimension of culture – values, beliefs, norms, habits, etc. – is important in understanding how the people perceive a technological innovation or new development project and assessing its consequences. The objectives of development projects may be more easily achieved if the experts are made aware of questions whose importance they fail to see because they take them as obvious and to which more importance needs to be given, for example, by educating members of the community.

Technological projects should strengthen regional and cultural identity by integrating traditional elements such as ritual and know-how at the planning and implementation stages. In addition, local manpower should be used and care taken to ensure that the community participates more in decision-making.

Ensuring that members of the benefiting community take part in the development project poses certain problems: motivating the people concerned, whose representation at the discussion and implementation phases needs to be balanced, and ensuring freedom of dialogue between them and the outside workers.

The introduction of a new technology in a society requires skills and methods under the headings of communication, interaction and education. Technological innovations and projects may have effects that are functional and/or dysfunctional, direct and/or indirect, apparent and/or latent, and immediate and/or long-term.

The causes of dysfunction have been studied. They are, first and foremost, the structure of the prevailing authority in the community and technological innovations. The experts themselves exerted a cultural influence on the local society and culture where they worked. Their comparatively luxurious lifestyle may have had an inflationary effect on and alienated the local community. The instruments used by research workers may also have a sociocultural dimension that would need to be taken into account.

THE GERMAN MINISTRY FOR ECONOMIC CO-OPERATION AND DEVELOPMENT

German action under the economic co-operation heading is part of a broader context of co-operation for the development of the countries of the South. A few years ago the ministry (Bundesministerium für Zusammenarbeit – BMZ) brought out a guide on the practical approach to and means of identifying cultural problems in the planning of development projects and programmes. But the guide was not taken into general use, particularly in the ministry's departments administering technical assistance and loans. Discussions on this subject are continuing.

In addition to the ministry itself there are several institutions working on the problems of the cultural dimension of development, including the German Foundation for International Development (Deutsche Stiftung für Internationale Entwicklung), the German Overseas Institute (Deutsches Übersee Institut), the Freiburg University Institute for Cultural Sciences Research and the Duisburg University Institute for Development and Peace. All these organizations frequently work on behalf of the Ministry for Co-operation and Development and the German development agencies, the latter including the German Agency for Technical Co-operation (Deutsche Gesellschaft für Technische Zusammenarbeit), the Central Agency for the Study of Foreign Cultures and Countries and the German Bank for Reconstruction and Development.

Non-governmental organizations

The role of non-governmental organizations (NGOs) in co-operation for development is paramount. This is partly due to their legal status (they do not come under public law) and to a large extent to their wide variety in size and field and in the level at which they operate. It is mainly in the form of lightweight structures and in work at ground level that they have a special role and are the most numerous. Over 5,000 officially recognized development aid NGOs are working in India, for example, while over 20,000 others have no official status but are just as active.

In addition to these countless field NGOs, large-scale organizations have been formed, examples being the Catholic Committee against Hunger and for Development (CCHD) and the Oxford Committee for Famine Relief (OXFAM). The drawbacks of their large size are offset by their power to act and their working methods: extensive breakdown of structures in OXFAM's case and indirect action via teams of fieldworkers ('getting done' rather than 'doing') in that of CCHD.

The work of NGOs, very different as it is from that of the large bilateral and multilateral co-operation agencies, is of considerable value primarily in terms of cultural sensitivity and the quality of the results achieved. In addition, the amounts that NGOs receive from governments and co-operation agencies are very much smaller than those allocated to programmes administered by the big organizations. Their success and the approach they take have had profound effects on large institutions such as the World Bank, ACDI, USAID, etc. In that respect the work of Grameen Bank in Bangladesh and Sarvodaya in Sri Lanka is regarded as exemplary.

OXFORD COMMITTEE FOR FAMINE RELIEF (OXFAM)

Set up in 1942 by a group of Oxford residents with the object of relieving poverty, distress and suffering throughout the world, OXFAM has gradually grown into one of the largest development aid NGOs. It lends its support, in the form of grants, to over 2,000 highly varied field agencies in over seventy countries. Over £61 million were distributed in 1992–93 for OXFAM activities overseas and on its education programme. The principles on which OXFAM action is based are the following:

(a) people themselves are able to overcome problems and the forces that oppress or exploit them;

(b) all human beings have the right to feed and house themselves and to enjoy reasonable living conditions;

(c) development, aimed above all and without discrimination at helping the very poorest, needs to be pursued by organizations and small local groups in such a way as to help people live with less difficulty and to encourage self-determination through recognition of their priorities and cultural models;

77

(d) OXFAM acts as a social micro-catalyst, helping small groups to face up to the oppressive factors of their environment and fight against them.

In order to put these principles into practice, OXFAM has produced a field guide for NGOs whose general objective and working methods are clearly of a sociocultural nature:

- acquiring knowledge about the area they work in, questioning one's own principles, accepting the validity of the 'unfamiliar' and getting to know: local languages; modes of social integration; the distribution of work and the impact of religion;
- questioning people themselves with tact and patience about what they are in order to win their confidence and establish quality human relations by listening to their comments, holding frank discussions with them and informing them of the results of the observations made;
- understanding such things as the social role of men and women and local forms of participation and of knowledge;
- working by stages with the local communities and planning for them to take over projects after the fieldworkers have gone;
- giving preference, in general, to research-action methods.

CATHOLIC COMMITTEE AGAINST HUNGER AND FOR DEVELOPMENT

The Catholic Committee against Hunger and Development (CCHD), a 'public interest' association under the patronage of the bishops of France, has a twofold mission: in the rich countries, to cultivate awareness of the importance and urgency of an ongoing policy of support for development; and, in the countries of the South, to finance and promote sustainable development projects with the aid of local managers, in particular in South America, Africa and South-East Asia. In 1991, CCHD financed and supported 677 development initiatives in eighty-six countries. While taking into account the diversity of local backgrounds and the specific characteristics of the fields of action, these projects are all based on the desire of the population concerned to take their own future in hand.

But the CCHD authorities consider that their action can only meet needs on this kind of scale if the countries of the North reflect and question themselves about their responsibility in regard to the development of those of the South. They believe that education in international fellowship is one of the priorities of our time. CCHD is planning to set up a foundation for the purpose, of which all the NGOs working in this field would be members.

THE CULTURES NETWORK

Another form of non-governmental action is represented by the Cultures Network, which brings together NGOs working in Africa, Asia, Europe and Latin America. The aim of the network is to provide a system of flexible communication, pooled research, training and mutual support involving individuals, NGOs, officials and academics, working in the countries of both the North and the South.

According to *Quid pro quo*, the network's newsletter, 'cultures are made up of values, symbols and forms of spirituality, social and political organizations, know-how and skills. In the face of the new challenges, social struggles and the need for change, people find in their culture a source of "alternatives" to the dominant development models, too closely identified with materialistic concepts, productivism and individualism and far too dependent on Western-style technocratic solutions.' There is a need for new approaches that take into account and reinforce the dynamic interaction between outside influences and local cultures.

The Cultures Network is unusual inasmuch as it is concerned both with field practice and with research into the problems of organic interaction between cultures, cultural factors and development. For example, in April 1992 it organized a method workshop on the cultural analysis of development projects at Nogent-le-Rotrou.

THE PANOS INSTITUTE

The Panos Institute, an independent international NGO consisting of four NGOs in France, Hungary, the United Kingdom and the United States, has been working on the problems of sustainable development since 1980 and more particularly on the distribution of information that is useful and accessible to all types of users involved in rescue and development projects in the field. The institute has also produced information programmes on the impact of migration and apartheid problems on development. Its main achievement, however, is the preparation of a guide on the use of techniques for collecting and applying the oral tradition in agricultural and pastoral practices and on the change in ecological conditions, traditional medicine and the norms governing social relations. The guide is based on interviews with over 500 old people, both men and women, in Sahel countries: Burkina Faso, Chad, Ethiopia, Mali, Mauritania, Niger, Senegal and Sudan. The methods proposed for the collection of data and their integration in project design and implementation could be used in other contexts, while allowing for cultural differences due to the climatic conditions, geographical situation and history of countries located in other parts of the world where this particular method could be applied.

CHAPTER 3

Progress and problems:
a balance sheet

Limits of progress achieved and need for new approaches and instruments

As we have seen, between the early 1970s and the present decade considerable progress has been made: firstly, in our understanding and awareness of the content of the concept of culture and development, which has found expression in particular in the emergence of the notion of a cultural dimension of development; secondly, in our ways of defining and approaching development problems and development co-operation, whatever form the latter may take. In various areas we have even begun to construct instruments for analysing and taking into account the cultural factors and cultural effects of development.

However, when it comes to entering into the very heart of cultural processes, which cannot be reduced to social processes or to the human aspects of development or to the notion of quality of life, we seem to have reached an ultimate limit beyond which we cannot go. These difficulties are of both a theoretical and a practical nature.

At the theoretical level, our thinking and proposals for scientific analysis need to be placed in a global perspective which, nevertheless, takes into account the reality of the world's cultural diversity and the constant exchanges and interactions between culture and other aspects of social life.

Firstly, the extension of the concept of culture to ways of life, value systems, knowledge and know-how demands a radical change in the approach to, objectives of and mechanisms for development. If we describe the work to be done in its different stages, taking the

81

psycho-sociological aspects of culture into account primarily requires an in-depth analysis of their components and concrete manifestations. In addition, it calls for the cultural factors thus identified to be ranged in hierarchical order, by picking out those which interact directly, and sometimes clash, with development values and objectives and which structure all the other factors. Lastly, it requires the players, factors, levels and fields of development, seen from a cultural angle, to be brought into dynamic and growing interaction.

In fact, as defined thirty years ago, development has shown itself to be not a neutral concept of universal application but attached to a specific type of society. Both experience and scientific research have shown that, in reality, it issued from the culture of industrial societies whose strategic factors and motivating values, as far as the market economy countries are concerned, are individualism (and its legal expression, human rights), competition, economic success, the twin virtues of organization and efficiency, and, finally, modernity. The communist ideology, for its part, preached mankind's pursuit of happiness by scientific progress, economic growth and the complete centralization of power in the hands of the state. Lastly, as we saw earlier, it is the same theory of development through accelerated economic growth that has long prevailed in the United Nations Organization itself.

· Thus, taking the cultural dimension into account in development means identifying, then 'operationalizing' and, finally, managing situations of conflict or compatibility between the cultures of the pre-industrial societies and the development culture, so as to encourage development that is both economic and human. Only on this condition will it be possible to provide the practical means of executing development projects whose economic success does not simultaneously jeopardize their human outcome. Within this context, it is possible correctly to assess progress and the limits of what has already been achieved with respect to the taking into account, at the theoretical and practical levels, of the non-economic factors of development and the new means to be devised for this purpose.

The progress represented by the emergence of new modes of conceptualizing development – sustainable development and human development – has already been described. These concepts open up certain prospects of taking the cultural dimension of development – that is, the cultural factors and effects of development – into account, but to some extent it is a question of concepts allied to that of the cultural dimension of development, some aspects of which they overlap without following all their implications for ways of planning and implementing development activities in general.

Indeed, despite the progress that they represent in our understanding of the problems of development, these two concepts fail to give an account of the truly cultural reality of human behaviour. Thus the two notions, which appear to treat the cultural dimension as a supplementary consideration, need to be explored further. Only further delving into the respective contents of the notions of sustainable development and human development will clearly reveal the extent to which, implicitly or not, they include the cultural components usually embraced by the term 'cultural dimension of development'.

Difficulties of a conceptual or scientific nature are not the only ones to prevent the cultural factors from being integrated into development. Paradoxically, the proclaimed intentions are often only very partially translated into the design or evaluation of actual projects. The reasons for this are of three kinds: firstly, the technical nature of the development project programming and evaluation documents; secondly, the scales of observation both of the situations concerned and of the activities undertaken; and, finally, the geographical, economic, social and cultural distance between the decision-makers and the population concerned.

Thus, an examination of the documents shows that the characteristics common to the various development strategies, policies, programmes and projects are frequently still as follows: predominance of the economic dimension, lack of flexibility in time-scale, budget, administrative procedures and setting of objectives, sectoral fragmentation of projects and reduction of the cultural aspects to education and the elimination of illiteracy.[1]

---

1. See H. Panhuys, E. Sizoo and T. Verhelst, *La prise en compte des facteurs culturels dans les projets de développement* [Taking Cultural Factors into Account in Development Programmes], Part 2: *Prise en compte des approches culturelles par les grandes agences de développement* [Acknowledgement of Cultural Approaches by the Leading Development Agencies], pp. 58–66, Paris, UNESCO, 1993. (UNESCO doc. CLT-93/WS/3.)

Clearly, the very nature of the project and programme documents makes it difficult to include significant cultural references, other than in the most indirect terms.

The institutions with a global mandate necessarily produce documents with a macro-economic or macro-social scale of observation. This scale presupposes a search for regularity rather than diversity. Moreover, its adoption leads to preference being given to the classical methods of planning and data quantification. Similarly, it stresses activities that can easily be audited, that is to say it leads inevitably to the adoption of an economic, technological and organizational approach.

As described above, the distance between the decision-makers and the target population concerned also determines the nature and content of the strategies, programmes and policies aimed at development for the benefit of the local people, in particular the poorest and least fortunate. At the same time, the information, though it may be accessible on the ground, may fail to reach the top of the institutional 'pyramid' where decisions are taken and strategies devised.[2]

Thus, the participation of the population in its own development never extends beyond purely local limits, the 'vertical' or institutional channels of communication either distorting some of the data from the field or watering it down *en route*. Finally, at the peak policy-making level there is no system for making use of the information which might filter through. Also, as we have already seen, it is sometimes felt that the specialized research and even the studies specifically commissioned by the development aid agencies introduce insurmountable complications for decision-makers, accustomed as they are to clarity in the economic or technical approach corresponding more closely to their professional and entrepreneurial culture. As a result, decision-makers consult their peers, and not the 'field', before determining their broad programme of future action.

2. D. Desjeux, *Dimension culturelle et aide à la décision* [The Cultural Dimension and Aid to Decision-making], Introduction, pp. 2–11, Paris, UNESCO, 1993.

New proposals

New approaches and instruments for incorporating the cultural factors into development are therefore both indispensable and difficult to devise. Thus, following an analysis of the strategic factors that confront each other in the encounters between these two types of cultures, it will be necessary to propose two main categories of instruments – methodological and instructive – designed for the practical 'management' of the resulting interactions.

The fact is that, although the limits imposed on integration by the major economic forces involved must be taken into account, fresh proposals can still be made, building on the initiatives already taken while moving cautiously ahead in three directions where innovation is absolutely necessary:

1. As regards the study of the cultural factors and the cultural impact of development, the description of the process of identifying and incorporating these factors, the interactions they control and the priorities of application which they entail.

2. The *devising of means, methods and instruments* that will place at the disposal of the development institutions and officials: (a) on the one hand, *practical tools* (analysis tables, indicators, methods for planning, implementing and evaluating the effects of development) that are relatively simple to use in order to identify clearly and in concrete situations the cultural factors capable of reinforcing or paralysing development; and (b) on the other hand, *instruments* for capturing the globality and complexity (especially sociocultural) of the context in which developmental action is taking place and the duration of the effects of development projects, so as to make it easier to take into account the cultural milieu in which the projects are set and in which the populations affected by the choices and actions of the developers actually live; these approaches and instruments should help them to adapt their working methods and attitudes accordingly.

3. A series of proposals for stimulating the cultural *training* and *awareness* of decision-makers and 'developers' and for encouraging the participation and effective involvement of the local population in the preparation, execution and evaluation of projects intended to improve their living conditions in a manner consistent with their own aspirations, abilities and living conditions.

85

It is therefore possible as of now, on the basis of what has already been learned, to propose a first provisional set of analytical tables and programming, evaluation and training tools which, together, will help create the conditions for a significant move forward in the quest for dynamic interactions between culture and development. However, only by actually making use of these methods in the design, execution and evaluation of development projects and programmes will it be possible to conduct a full-scale test of the validity of the proposals made here and, where necessary, correct and improve them.

PART TWO

Cultural factors and cultural impact of development

Introduction

As we have seen, the importance of culture, in the sense of the ways of life, modes of thought and behaviour of the different peoples of the world, is more and more widely recognized and, in many cases, taken specifically into account by development officials. Thus, there have been references to the need to have regard for cultural identities, to have the population participate in their own development projects and to grant them the right of access to culture. However, in most cases these are isolated, often superficial references with only sketchy links with the question of the aims and processes of development itself. In short, in most cases, the reality of culture in all its diversity continues to be an aspect that is neglected more often than not by decision-makers and fieldworkers.

Accordingly, it will be necessary to undertake a systematic in-depth study of the cultural factors and the cultural impact of development. The first requirement will be to show how these factors can be identified and what part they play in development. The next step must be to analyse the values of development considered as a culture: is the final objective purely economic or is development rather a means of enabling humanity to blossom? Culture and development must then be envisaged in the light of their full range of interactions, if integrated development, in which culture takes its rightful place, is to be encouraged. Finally, it will have to be shown how this interaction operates in the specific areas of economic and social development.

CHAPTER 4

How cultural factors may be identified and taken into account

The definition of culture adopted at the Mexico City Conference and mentioned earlier states that the constituent elements of a culture consist of the whole complex of distinctive features that characterize a society or social group. It also says that these features may be spiritual, intellectual, material or emotional. Of the characteristics of a given culture, some are capable of having a positive or negative effect on development, thereby contributing to the final result and therefore needing to be identified and taken into account.

Within this global formulation, felt by some to be too broad, the definition in the Mexico Declaration on Cultural Policies distinguishes, at a narrower level:[1]

• traditions and beliefs;
• fundamental rights of the human being;
• value systems;
• modes of life;
• arts and letters.

Even these subdivisions and distinctions are still formulated in very general terms. Moreover, all these categories aim to describe specific aspects of cultures, except for the concept of human rights which may be regarded as a universal requirement (cf. the Universal Declaration of Human Rights), and that of 'arts and letters', which is restricted to the idea of the culture of the 'cultured'. Accordingly, if we wish to establish their place and their role in the development

---

1. UNESCO, *Mexico City Declaration on Cultural Policies*, Preamble (final report of Mondiacult: World Conference on Cultural Policies, Mexico City, 26 July to 6 August 1982), Paris, UNESCO, 1982. (UNESCO doc. CLT/MD/1.)

process, we shall have to analyse in greater detail the significance and content of the terms employed above by asking a number of questions. Is it possible for all traditions and beliefs to interact with development? Is it mainly religious beliefs that interact? Do aesthetic, ethical and spiritual values have the same influence in all societies? Are modes of life wholly unalterable or can some aspects of them be easily changed?

It is this last question that seems to be the most crucial, given the changes of all kinds that are taking place across the globe. What it does is to pose the question of change – affecting not only cultures and the pace of life but also forms of development. That being so, what we have to establish is whether all or only some of the components of the various cultures play the part of factors, that is active features of development in a positive or a negative sense. The following analysis must therefore be applied in a dynamic perspective, in other words set in the context of the interactions described at a later stage of the present study.

The analysis has therefore to include the following specific elements and aspects:

- · the rate at which cultural factors are changing (slow or fast);
- their order of importance, with identification of the major structure-forming elements and the strategic factors in relation to the confrontation with development values;
- the cultural aspects of social interactions;
- interactions between developers, the cultural and non-cultural factors of development and the levels and fields of action;
- the cultural impact of economic, social and technical development;
- the priority areas of application: cultural factors and cultural impact of development policies and projects in the economic (enterprises, monetary economy, saving, agriculture, informal sector) and social fields (basic education, health, food/nutrition, housing and urban development, population, women's role in development).

The research to be carried out in this field will not have an academic aim; its purpose will be rather to assist with decision-making and preparation for action. Consequently, while use will be made of existing anthropological, sociological and historical studies, the results will also be drawn from field observations and their interpretation.

Slow and fast variables

In the factors of continuity and change, each culture possesses a set of descriptive indicators that exist within a historical perspective, in relation to the past and the future.

These factors are subject to different rates of change. Some may be regarded as very long-term variables or even invariants, constituting, as it were, the cultural foundations and end goals of society, and change rapidly only in the event of radical economic or political upheavals. By contrast, other factors evolve much more rapidly, for example certain consumer fashions.

Two categories of factors may be distinguished: on the one hand, those that constitute the heritage and the history of a society (its continuity), and, on the other, the intrinsic creative elements and elements of change it contains. These are the elements that must be taken into consideration when attempting to assess the extent to which culture and development are compatible:

Continuity factors (or slow variables):

- traditions, beliefs, value systems and social, family, legal, ethical and spiritual norms, institutions and power structures;
- modes of life, ways of thought and production, practices, customs, distribution of functions and tasks, eating habits;
- events experienced as cultural in their own right: festivals, historical or religious celebrations, for example;
- languages and other forms of non-physical heritage.

Factors of change (or fast variables):

- needs and aspirations of the people, survival strategies;
- knowledge (science) and know-how (technologies, modes of social, political and economic organization, management of the environment, natural and man-made, medicine, etc.);
- creativity and ability to innovate;
- spoken language (in particular ways of speaking and vocabulary, mainly in urban areas and particularly under the influence of the media, with generation-related differences);
- technology transfers and intercultural communications, economic exchanges and trade;
- migration;
- changes to the environment.

Fast or slow, the rates of change of these groups of cultural characteristics can respond to various internal and external factors, gener-

93

ally of an economic and/or political nature, especially in the present international context, where it is possible to observe very rapid, sometimes even violent change in many situations.

The result is internal modifications affecting every type of variable and evolutionary disparities which may create conflict between societies and even within the same society (changes in styles of dress/traditions and customs, for example).

These continuity factors and factors of change determine the nature of the relations between individuals and the economy, the government and therefore development. In fact, in every culture they operate like a system of crisis indicators.

Thus, every culture includes a series of dynamic components which can work either for or against development objectives for periods and in forms that are hard to predict. This explains the frequent disparity between the planning of a project and its execution, conditioned by the pattern of life of the people concerned.

At the same time, if their nature and rate of change are not duly taken into account by the developers, the slow variables, to the extent that they represent the historical roots and, as it were, the 'substrate' of the culture, may act as brakes on development, especially if planned and controlled from the outside.

Thus, as we shall see later, the notions of invariants (or slow variables) and fast variables must be relativized if we are to understand cultures in a dynamic perspective. Tradition is not the whole of the past but only a part of it consisting of 'frozen movement', the result of deliberate choices endorsed by subsequent generations over a relatively long period. Conversely, the fast variables, in some cases experienced as 'culture shock' by the population or certain groups within it, may momentarily become powerful cultural symbols (clothing, for example) and 'crystallize' the refusal to accept certain aspects of change.

Cultural aspects of social divisions

Contrary to certain overgeneralized or outmoded approaches, it is not possible to speak of the culture of a society without making reference to the differences, sometimes acute, that pervade it and make culture the focus of power clashes that affect society as a whole. Whereas the culture often constitutes a rallying point in relation to the outside world, especially in situations of intercultural conflict, it does not perform the same role within the society itself. In reality, every culture is criss-crossed by social divisions – between age-groups, between the sexes, between town and country, between tradition and modernity – and by profound symbolic differences, accentuated more or less deliberately by their geographical or social proximity. These differences and the power relationships they represent tend to put into perspective overgeneralized analyses that would throw a cloak of uniformity over the distinctive detail of a culture. The latter may simply be that of the dominant group at a particular period. It is therefore necessary to qualify and relativize the correlation between certain specific cultural characteristics and the groups whose identity they express.

The problem of extreme poverty, in both the industrialized (fourth world) and the developing countries, especially the least advanced among them, obviously includes specific cultural factors and effects. The persistence of a culture may appear to be bound up with poverty itself, as a response to the economic distress of the population, at least up to the point at which the extremes of want destroy even the most basic values. Taken together, these elements of differentiation are of vital importance for identifying the target populations when development projects are being prepared, particularly when referring to the least economically developed countries.

Identification of the role of the major factors in the structuring of cultural values and norms[2]

The components of a culture are structurally interrelated in a manner that reveals their deep significance. Most of the time these features remain more or less implicit, even unmentioned. They are only openly and indeed ostentatiously displayed in conflict situations or on solemn occasions. Some of them become 'strategic' elements in the encounter or confrontation between the various pre-industrial cultures and the development culture.

2. X. Dupuis, *Contribution à l'étude des méthodes d'intégration des facteurs culturels dans le développement* [Contribution to the Study of Methods for Integrating Cultural Factors into Development], Paris, UNESCO, 1993.

In fact, in the face of change, each culture defines implicit and explicit hierarchies of consent, which determine the acceptability of development action. Thus, attitudes and aptitudes are the elements that control the permanence and transformation of cultures.

Some of these elements have a decisive influence on whether others survive, flourish or disappear. Thus, there is a hierarchy of cultural values which largely determines their compatibility (or potential for conflict) with development values and in which traditions, beliefs, value systems and norms play a fundamental role. It is in terms of these elements that, within a given time-frame, populations are able to decode the components of development projects, reinterpret them and make them their own.

BELIEFS AND NATURE

Against this background it is possible to distinguish two principal factors: beliefs and nature or, more precisely, the natural milieu, whether or not modified by man. These may be regarded as structure-building in the sense that they determine value systems, social and economic organization, modes of life and forms of intellectual and aesthetic expression.

Interacting with the political, economic and social structures, they create the framework of every society, that is to say its 'world-view', value system and norms.

However, the interaction between beliefs and nature is not simply deterministic, as evidenced by the development of different cultures in environments with the same geographical characteristics (an island environment, for example), but may take highly varied forms depending on historical background.

Beliefs should be understood to include the religions, popular cults (such as ancestor worship), ordered rites and practices of a sacred and symbolic nature, traditions (ways of thinking, doing and behaving inherited from the past) and customs (collective habits passed on from generation to generation). Beliefs constitute the heart of a people's cultural experience. The mystical dimension, what they consider 'sacred', forms the basis of their view of the world, the meaning of life, the relation between past and future, their value systems and, indirectly, their social structures, behaviour and attitudes. For their part, the traditions and customs reflect the continuity of society, its ways of dealing with the critical moments of life, and the distinction between normality and what is forbidden.

It is primarily the system of beliefs, forms of worship, rituals, traditions and customs which expresses the relationship between life and death, regulates the stages of life, draws the lines between what is desirable, what is permissible and what is forbidden and makes sense of human endeavour in the material, intellectual, spiritual and ethical spheres. There is no society without guiding values and, depending on whether or not these values correspond to a transcending of the mundane, in the sense of a purely spiritual accomplishment, or the achievement of spiritual ends by acting upon the reality of the world as it exists, this system of principles and standards can serve to accelerate or hold back development, understood in the economic sense, but especially in the sense of an improvement in living conditions for all, driven by these values and based on respect for what they represent for a given population.

Values of this type stand in clear contrast to the purely materialistic values whose hold over modern societies is regularly deplored. However, to the extent that they require a human influence to be exerted on society and the natural milieu, they can clearly work in synergy with the spirit and logic of development.

Nature (or the natural milieu) is the second decisive element in the constitution of a culture since it is, in part, the resultant of the interaction between the community and its environment. It is therefore essential to take fully into account the relations between all the members of a group and the water, earth, air, flora and fauna that constitute their ecological heritage, while also forming part of their economic (crop and animal farming, hunting and fishing) and cultural heritage. The cultural tradition of every community includes precise ideas about the environment, the legacy of previous generations. The relationship with nature is imbued with interpretations and myths. It is the product of beliefs and/or accumulated experience of the functioning of the universe and the roles of groups and individuals in the management of natural resources. For instance, the West African peasant perceives nature to be both useful and sacred: no sentimentalism with respect to the vegetable kingdom, no ecological conscience, but a close intermeshing of man and environment. Trees are never ornaments. They perform all sorts of useful functions: economic (as a source of food or raw materials, for example the acacia in the savannahs of Sudan and the Sahel), climatic (as a regulator of the micro-climate), even legal (the presence of a tree determines the ownership of the field in which it is planted). The tree also has a religious function: for the Sereras of Senegal trees are the dwelling places of the ancestral spirits.[3]

This religious function of trees may be compared with the spiritual dimension of the use made of forests in South and South-East Asia (see FIPC/FAO project, Part 1, p. 61).

The cultural tradition also includes a set of knowledge acquired collectively which, in various ecosystems, enables natural resources to be conserved and regenerated (for example, in rural development certain agricultural techniques used to be employed to reclaim land that had become infertile). However, this knowledge is always underlain by a supernatural dimension of the natural. In Indonesia, for example, the relationship between man and nature is conceived by the various communities of the archipelago within a context strongly influenced by the various religions which have been successively practised by the local populations (Buddhism, Christianity, Hinduism and Islam). Nature plays a preponderant role in the communities of the archipelago where man is considered subordinate to nature. The biophysical forces (such as volcanic eruptions, the ability of the land to yield rice or the sea to provide fish) even now form part of a system of beliefs, particularly for the rural population. Only very recently, in fact, in one of the communities of the Moluccan archipelago, a sort of local police supervised the observance of certain unwritten laws such as 'Sasi', an environmental code which, at local level, prohibits fishing in the rivers during the breeding season.[4]

However, the perception of nature as an inexhaustible 'foster-mother' has also led some peoples to resort to destructive practices such as *tavy* (slash and burn) and overgrazing in Madagascar. These practices, appropriate for small groups living off large territories, are harmful when the population increases sharply, with no increase in territory, and is unable to adapt to the resulting conditions. This is what has happened, for example, to certain populations in the Sahel. Moreover, in some tropical countries the intensive exploitation of forest resources, for strictly economic reasons, may lead to irreversible ecological and cultural destabilization.

3. J.-M. Gastellu, *L'arbre ne cache pas la forêt: ou usus, fructus et abusus* [Seeing the Wood for the Trees], ORSTOM Notebooks, Human Sciences Series, Vol. XVII, Nos. 3–4, 1980.
4. Quoted by Dupuis, op. cit.

SOCIAL AND POLITICAL NORMS AND STRUCTURES

Clearly, social and political norms and structures lie at the heart of a highly dialectical relationship, since they are both constituents and consequences of culture. They are a reflection of the value systems. In this respect, a sense of individual identity is crucial. The family, political and also economic behaviour of the individual will vary, depending on his feeling of belonging to a group and on the social pressure or even coercion applied by the group (family, tribe, ethnic community, nation). In this connection, legal practices are of vital importance.

This is the level at which disputes are settled between leader groups and other cultural, social or ethnic groups, within the same political entity, and where the problems of caring for the weak, handicapped and variously marginalized are – or are not – solved. It is also the level at which it is decided whether to cling to former ways (tradition or routine) or actively to accept innovation, economic, social or technological. In this context, discussion and negotiations will be of overriding importance.

At a more general level, the persistence of norms and structures raises the question of fundamental human rights, which form an integral part of any culture, as reiterated in the Mexico City Declaration on Cultural Policies. According to the Universal Declaration of Human Rights, these rights are as follows: 'life, liberty and security of person; recognition as a person before the law; freedom of thought, conscience and religion; protection of the law against interference with privacy, family, home or correspondence and attacks against honour; the right to seek asylum from persecution; the right to a nationality; the right to marry and found a family; the right to own property'. Clearly, these universal principles receive very different 'interpretations' from one society to another.

Thus, this question brings us to the more general problem of the power structure within a given community or society. In a sense, as a unifying element, the culture of a society is that of the group which exercises political, economic and spiritual power over it. In relation to the latter, the other social groups are in a position of dependence (patronage), dialogue (networks of influence) or more or less open conflict. Accordingly, the culture of these groups may differ profoundly from that of the group in power. Moreover, depending on the society in question, there may be networks of 'complicity' (clans, ethnic or family ties, brotherhoods, 'clubs' and professional and hobby groups). This type of social relationship can exert a powerful influence on the implementation of development strategies, for example, strategies for integration in the world economy.

One of the most impressive aspects of cultures is the way in which, from ancient times, bodies of oral or written customary law are built up. These are compendia of principles and norms of varying sophistication, which make it possible to regulate the general functioning of society, control the means of exercising power, resolve conflicts between individuals and between groups, and organize activities of every kind: family, social, economic, educational, religious and sporting. Almost always rooted in religion and expressed as custom, its experts being the upholders of tradition, in many societies the law has gradually assumed the form of written legislation based on rational principles, having lost contact with its religious origins. Moreover, in principle, certain tenets of the law concerning respect for the person, enshrined in the Universal Declaration of Human Rights, apply everywhere and in all circumstances (see above). But there are many countries where written and customary law coexist. For instance, in Cameroon, as in many other countries, written law is backed up by customary law, under which the sages in possession of traditional knowledge are convened, whenever necessary, as a recognized body whose judgements are taken into account by the higher authorities. This is the case, in particular, where the law of landed property is concerned: the obtaining of a title to land always involves the holding of a 'palaver', which ends in a verdict on the legitimacy of ownership reached in the light of the traditional law of succession and inheritance. In such matters the keepers of tradition are perfectly competent, since, in general, inheritance is regulated and its legitimacy sanctioned by colleges of patriarchs. Thus, the Cameroonian civil code lays great store by customary law and traditional legislation in general.[5]

The place and role of men and women in society, some aspects of which hark back to the most distant past, are closely bound up with religion but also with the family and social environment, property, power structures, the organization of production and relations

5. Quoted by Dupuis, op. cit.

with the body (link and distinction to be made between the maternal function and mastery of the body). Their tasks, their role, their influence on family and community decisions, their rights over persons and goods and, in general, their participation in economic and social life are linked with the system of relationships (precedence among descendants, rights of the eldest) and number among the essential characteristics of a culture. For example, an inquiry into the poor attendance at health centres in the Kisii district of Kenya showed that in the design and execution of the programme insufficient attention had been paid to sociocultural factors. When asked why they were not making use of these centres, the women usually gave pretexts (they had too much to do, had nothing suitable to wear, or the centres were too far away to get there on foot with their children). Although the majority of the women – for the most part mothers of eight or nine children – obviously wanted to know more about how to space out their pregnancies, the husbands and mothers-in-law were opposed to any form of contraception. However, the women were more afraid of being sterile than of being too fertile. As a result of the inquiry, the programme was reoriented to ensure that the husbands and mothers-in-law were also informed about family planning. This feeling is very strong among certain Bantu populations who believe that the dead remain behind as spirits to watch over and guide the other members of their family. However, if there are no offspring, all contact is lost. This belief explains the frequent repudiation of childless women.[6]

The balance between the respective roles of women and men is particularly important in styles of organization, behaviour and values in the family. As the primary group structure in all societies, it is within the family that the individual's relations with the community and those between generations take shape as a result of the blood relationship. The group may consist of the enlarged family, almost the clan, in traditional societies or be simply the nuclear family

6. See P. Dugue and J.-M. Jung, 'Reconstruction de la fertilité: Kenya, Yabunga, Burkina Faso [Reconstruction of Fertility: Kenya, Yabunga, Burkina Faso]', *Le développement humain*, p. 49, quoted by L. Augustin-Jean, *Contribution à la synthèse méthodologique sur l'intégration des facteurs culturels au développement* [Contribution to the Methodological Synopsis of the Integration of Cultural Factors in Development], Paris, UNESCO, 1993.

comprising only parents and children, as is most often the case in modern societies.

The predominant family model plays an important part in social, economic and political life: what some call family solidarity others brand as nepotism or even clientelism. Conversely, the quality of relations between parents and children very much depends on the intellectual and moral preparation of young people for the difficulties of adult life. Lastly, at the level of the community or society, the transmission of culture and in particular of values and language depends as much on instruction within the family as on school and non-school education outside the family (note here that mothers everywhere have a paramount role in teaching children the language of their community or country). Anthropological and sociological observation demonstrates that the role assigned to women (daughters-in-law) in the traditional family, organized around a common forebear and including the male descendants and their immediate family, is fixed and restricted to domestic functions and motherhood, including care of small children and their early instruction, generally under the eye of the husband's mother and sisters. On reaching adolescence, children come under the responsibility of the male members of the clan in respect of all matters pertaining to social life (initiation), returning to the mother only in crisis situations, for instance in case of war. Conversely, the nuclear family (parents and their children) has resulted in the educational system taking over at an increasingly early age the initiation of children in regard to life and social values. However, the mother/child relationship is still frequently modelled along traditional lines, not to speak of the organic link maintaining a special relationship between the two.

ECONOMIC NORMS

Just as every society produces a culture, among the numerous rules and systems that control its functioning every culture contains economic norms relating to the production, marketing and consumption of goods and services and to the constitution and preservation of its heritage in the widest (economic but also cultural and natural) sense. In all the processes at work in this field these norms govern the role and modes of action of the various groups of which society is made up: each of its members, bearer of the culture of that society, is at the same time imprinted with the rules that determine his or her role in the fellowships or collective actions that serve this purpose.

Thus, the status of the land, which is still the principal means of production in many developing countries, is closely bound up with cultural references: in the allocation of land, in the systems of land use, and also in the management of the environment. In fact, every society has its 'nature reserves' which, depending on the circumstances, may take the form of 'sacred groves' or be the territory of the spirits, the dead or the gods and are therefore never subjected to any form of economic exploitation (see the FAO project for forest exploitation in South-East Asia, p. 61).

Moreover, the ownership, individual or common, of the land leads to methods of land utilization (grazing or crop cultivation) which have a profound influence on the mode and rhythm of life of the population and must be analysed and taken carefully into account when one type of activity is substituted for another (cattle-breeding for crop farming, cash-crop for subsistence farming) or new methods of agriculture are introduced.

The other means of production – tools, utensils, craftsman's instruments – also comply with rules which are all the more precise in societies that can be described as 'traditional'. Every 'profession' has its status and corresponding degree of prestige, and the resulting diversification of tasks has deep cultural roots. The same applies to the organization of labour, and this aspect too must be examined with particular care when work is transferred into a new context: that of the co-operative enterprise or large-scale institutional structure.

Another element to be taken into account is the status of labour, viewed either as a short-term effort with immediate and satisfying returns or as a medium- or long-term process, whose technical effects will become apparent only after a relatively long delay, at the end of a long trail of sacrifice and endeavour, with expectation of immediate results or 'gratification' placed more or less entirely 'on the back burner'. Alienation at work can be best accepted if the meaning of the effort demanded is well understood and endorsed by the population concerned. Thus, it must be appreciated that a development project often entails extra effort on the part of the population and that that effort will not be forthcoming unless the groups involved in the project consider it to be in their interest. This is one of the most important ways of motivating the population for development activities as a whole.

Moreover, work being both a cultural and a social activity, its practice and logic are not always and everywhere governed by the same rules, which brings us to another notion fundamental to development: the perception of time, which is that of the people doing the work. For example, in India,

in 1961, a hundred or so women were engaged in moving earth to clear temples and, to the astonished Western traveller, the way they worked seemed totally irrational. Each woman picked up a basket of stones, carried it four or five metres on her head, and then put it down for the next woman to come and pick up in her turn. For a European observer, the waste of energy was scandalous. . . . However, on reflection, it became clear that . . . the village was not 'working' but engaging in a social activity. . . .[7]

The same applies to the maintenance of collectively owned equipment: intrinsically foreign by origin, where international co-operation projects are concerned, it cannot be 'appropriated' by the population until the latter has been properly taught to appreciate it. Such action should preferably be carried out in a context of experimental participation of the beneficiary community in the preparation and execution of each operation, whose data and norms it has to translate via its own cultural coding system.

It is this entire system of elements which needs to be taken into account in the design and execution of development projects, in particular by analysing their possible synergetic effects and, on the other hand, their potential for setting back the project or even provoking conflict. These observations apply equally to projects in the public and private sectors and those at local, national and international levels. In fact, choices and strategies are still most often based on the logic of short-term profitability or the rules of good administrative management of public loans. They result in the project being evaluated only in relation to the programme and not in an analysis of its direct and indirect economic, social and cultural effects, except perhaps in quantitative terms.

Trading is governed by rules that are precise in space and time,

7. See J. Austruy, *Le scandale du développement* [Development Scandal], Paris, Clairefontaine, 1987.

and is most strikingly embodied in markets and fairs. But trading is also regulated by the value placed on the goods traded, either in a barter transaction or by translation into money terms, fixed or nego-tiable. For many societies, bargaining is one of their most ancient commercial traditions. It is one of the common cultural characteris-tics of the Mediterranean area, for example.

On the other hand, transition to a money economy with its de-rivatives, saving and lending, involves a series of profound cultural changes, especially for the rural populations in some regions of the world. In this area, therefore, the pace of change can only be very slow.

The notion of spending is itself an eminently cultural one. It does not merely represent the rational investment of a sum of money or effort in the acquisition of goods or services whose value has been carefully assessed. It also involves excess and the brushing aside of the rules and constraints of everyday life. In this respect, it has much in common with the holiday, a 'red-letter' day set apart from the rest. Depending on the society, practices as diverse as reli-gious sacrifice, games of chance or attempts to gain entry to the spirit world by artificial means (alcohol, hallucinogens, etc.) can be viewed in this light.

In many societies (Western as well as African, Asian or Native American), the poorest elements do not hesitate to spend lavishly on ceremonies such as weddings and funerals, going into debt for several years, if necessary. This type of spending, familiar to anthro-pologists as *potlatch*, clearly does not correspond to any modern no-tion of rational economic behaviour, but is of considerable symbolic importance to the family that engages in it, in the eyes of the com-munity to which it belongs and for that community as a whole. It harks back to traditions and beliefs firmly rooted in the culture of the population concerned. The case of the Kwakiutl population on the north-west coast of North America, between Vancouver and Alaska, is especially significant. Thus, it comprises festivities that have a religious connotation, with distributions and sometimes ex-change of gifts – and even destruction of these – generally to ce-ment matrimonial links and aiming too at a type of redistribution of wealth and enhancement of the social status of the donors.[8]

8. See Drucker and Heitzer, *A Re-examination of the Southern Kwakiutl Potlatch*, Berkeley, Calif., Berkeley University Press, 1988.

Conversely, the extreme poverty of some populations – para-doxically – gives rise to modes of life and expressions of solidarity which cannot be clearly accounted for in purely economic terms. Thus, in this case it is especially important to take a cultural ap-proach to development initiatives aimed at these populations and to pay particular attention to so-called 'informal' activities (see below).

Saving and lending and, more generally, the ways of accumulat-ing and managing wealth lie at the heart of development processes. Shaped by the culture, they define different types of relationships to ownership (of land, resources and wealth) and determine the atti-tude to money and hence to saving. In this respect, the example of saving habits can be illuminating.

The shortage of savings in the developing countries is a prob-lem commonly considered to be endemic. Confronted with the heavy burden of external debt, which is making it increasingly im-perative for some countries to generate themselves the savings needed for their own development, the banks are constantly seeking ways of overcoming the enormous difficulties of enlarging their cus-tomer base, especially in the rural areas, and gathering in more funds, which they can then pass on in the form of loans. Now, because of the guarantees it demands (for instance from a relative or next of kin), the banking system is ill-suited for mobilizing sav-ings and, more particularly, for granting loans to the rural popula-tion and small urban enterprises.

Accordingly, in the cities savings are collected by informal bank-ers. At the same time, the lack of collateral available to the peasants, who have low incomes and often do not own the land they till, has discouraged the banks from increasing their loans to poor or landless farmers. Only officials and merchants are able to obtain loans. This is the background to efforts aimed at mobilizing savings to be made available to the peasants. In this connection, one might mention the efforts of NGOs to set up 'savings and loans banks' for the benefit of poor villagers and the innovative experiments of the Grameen Bank (see p. 132 below).

At the same time, most countries have their savers. The main problems are, on the one hand, keeping the savings at home in the form of local investments, and, on the other, mobilizing them and directing them towards development projects. It is here that the banks tend to be largely ineffective. Their failure is due to the man-ner in which the banking system is set up, without adaptation to local conditions, without regard for the specific behaviour of the local people who even today continue to manage their heritage in the traditional way.

Because of the way they work, the classical commercial banks cannot cater to the needs of the rural population and the informal sector. They run up against the sensitive problem of loan guarantees and collateral which small farmers cannot provide. Accordingly, several systems have been set up to facilitate access to credit, and thereby enhance the development potential of the populations concerned. Those described below have proved successful in a number of cases and under certain conditions. They all presuppose familiarity with the local potential.

Tontines, named after the Neapolitan banker, Lorenzo Tonti, have a very long history. They are found in regions as diverse as Africa and Asia and have long been known in Europe.

In French-speaking Africa the tontine is an association of people paying a regular amount into a joint fund drawn out by each member when his turn comes.

The complex tontines differ from the simple ones in that they pay a variable interest which determines the shares received by the participants. The interest may either be deducted from the total amount or added to subsequent repayments, given to the participants or held in a solidarity fund. The mode of operation of some of these tontines is fixed in every detail. Thus, the rules governing a tontine that was practised in China in the 1930s, in the coastal province of Chejiang with its trading tradition, specified the periodicity of meetings, the rotation and amount of the contributions, the role of the guarantors, the posting of the operation in US dollars and even the cost of the meal served during the meeting. It is this type of tontine that is used in the Chinese diaspora both in Asia and in Europe.[9]

9. L. Augustin-Jean, op. cit.

Knowledge, know-how and technologies

TRADITION AND INNOVATION

Over the centuries, every culture, every society has built up a body of technical and practical expertise, which is still being enriched. Some of this derives from an attempted general and comprehensive interpretation of the world, while some meets the need to organize knowledge and know-how somewhat along the lines of the various Western scientific disciplines. The fairly widespread dissemination of such knowledge and the existence of reserved pools of know-how in both traditional and modern societies result in cultural divisions, which are very often social divisions as well.

Thus, the systems of family or social education, in or out of school, and the modes, traditional or modern, of initiation into and transfer of knowledge (written or oral tradition, organization according to sex or caste, but also secrets and taboos, etc.) also have a decisive influence on cultures and their transmission. Although continuity is thereby ensured, the field of education is, at the same time, an area of confrontation with new values and new knowledge, generally of outside origin as far as the developing countries are concerned.

It is also necessary to dispel a too common error concerning the fundamental inequality of written and oral cultures. The inability to read or write in no way signifies a lack of knowledge. In many cultures, oral traditions are just as important as the written word as a means of passing on the intellectual heritage. Better use should be made of the riches they represent in harnessing all the vital forces of a community to the development process.

While all societies generate knowledge, they also possess a store of know-how, i.e. technologies, in fields as diverse as medicine, farming, nutrition, building, personal hygiene and public health. These are cultural resources whose importance cannot be overestimated.

Unfortunately, especially in the 1970s, in many developing countries confusion arose between technological transformation and local technological development. The incoherent policies and *laissez-faire* in the technology field that ensued in some cases led to the underutilization of the national scientific and technological potential. Other countries embarked on large-scale projects divorced

108

from any overall economic strategy. These projects had a negative effect on the environment while discrediting local cultural experience and know-how. At the same time, the culture of a community is to a large extent the basis of the self-confidence it needs to take charge of its own development. One World Bank project, for example, concerned improving local irrigation in the Philippines. Unfortunately a preliminary feasibility study had overlooked the local traditional associations known as *zanjeras*. As a result, a first test carried out on a pilot zone was met with vigorous resistance from the people concerned, attributable to the social organization of the *zanjeras*. In this system each peasant tills a number of separate plots, this arrangement being designed to ensure that each person shares equally in the water. The first person to use the water cannot afford to waste it without imperilling the irrigation of his other plots downstream. The system is backed up by a very precise sharing arrangement governing everyone's rights and duties and the settlement of disputes.

Unfortunately this system had been left out of account when the project was set up and, because only the technical problems had been considered, the specialists planned for new irrigation ditches without making any allowance for the existing structure.[10]

Similarly, among the Guarani populations of Paraguay, thirty years of innovation have undermined the cohesion of the villages, sown doubt in the minds of the villagers (thus paralysing individual initiative), reduced the ability of the various groups to manage the resources of their natural environment and aggravated the disparities between big and small farmers. Previously, the peasants used swamp water to flood the rice paddies and water resources were managed by an informal users' association, which took care of distribution and maintained the canals. The replacement of oxen by tractors, the rise of the agro-industry and recourse to irrigation to permit modern farming on vast tracts of land have led to the pauperization of the small farmer.[11]

10. M. Cernea, *Putting People First: Sociological Variables in Rural Development*, Washington, D.C., World Bank/Oxford University Press, 1985.
11. R. Fogel, *La cultura y la gestión del agua en el Paraguay* [Culture and Water Management in Paraguay], Paris, UNESCO, 1991. (UNESCO doc. WS/CLT/DEC/CD/07.)

In the face of such examples, it must be acknowledged that the expansion of Western technology is mainly driven by a powerful economic incentive, the desire to make profits. Accordingly, it calls into question the local know-how, distribution of wealth, and social organization of the community. The participation of the population is only rarely effective and the transfer of technology is generally only partially successful. Nevertheless, the economic projects of the developing countries nearly always involve the virtually unconditional adoption of the hypothesis of development based exclusively on technology transfer and mass industrialization.

This is a mistake which can have serious consequences: unless the training of human resources is tackled by specific large-scale measures, technology transfer means no more than the mere importation of foreign equipment, techniques and technicians. This leads inexorably to the progressive marginalization of the local population, thus aggravating their loss of self-confidence. Moreover, Western techniques may prove ill-suited to local realities. In Africa, for example, modern Western architecture has often replaced traditional buildings made of mud, which is cheaper than concrete and better suited to the African climate, social structures and traditional art forms. To take an example, a major project – 'Global Development in New Human Settlements' – now in progress in Egypt involves the creation of new agricultural areas and the irrigation of desert land for which the provision of new villages is necessary. New forms of housing are therefore being designed, inspired by the ideas of Hassan Fatih, the great Egyptian architect and promoter of the idea of development for and by the local people and not imposed from outside. Among other things, the project includes the adaptation of traditional architectural styles and old building methods and materials to the new housing areas and to urban construction itself. The operation also makes use of the traditional know-how and skills of building workers and includes the creation of jobs for the local population, for example in agriculture, crafts and traditional forms of trade.

Finally, and all too often, the training received by the local élite further reinforces the belief in Western-style development. Trainees are intimately involved in the implementation of development plans and just as closely tied to the industrialized countries by material interest and cultural imitation. Educated in the universities of the former colonizers or in turnkey models which the latter export, they are in fact steeped in foreign value systems and largely formed in the Western mould. Accordingly, the members of these élites have a natural tendency to cling to the idea of progress as defined in the West. They are, in fact, its natural allies.

Furthermore, this trend raises the question of the attitude of the population to innovation. Traditional societies, which are supposed necessarily to reject innovation, and modern societies, supposedly in constant evolution, are too often considered to be mutually exclusive. In fact, every type of society is capable of innovation. However, the application of new technologies, endogenous or exogenous, depends on numerous parameters and, in particular, on the risk factor.

Thus the International Co-operation Centre of Agricultural Research for Development (CIRAD) has shown that, over the last thirty years, numerous innovations could be successfully introduced in the Sudan–Sahel belt. Their utilization often depends on the vagaries of the climate, national policies, the international economic environment and the risks to which the peasants are exposed. In the groundnut-growing region of Senegal, several innovations have been introduced: seed selection, mechanized sowing and weeding, and mineral fertilizer. These changes were readily adopted by the peasantry, as they involved only minimal risk. For example, with mineral fertilizer the technical and economic risks are limited. However, orders fluctuated with economic conditions (the fertilizer/groundnut price ratio, for example). At the same time, the project demonstrated the producers' willingness to invest, despite a difficult economic context, when they were sure of their cash markets. Thus, an articulated production-centred credit/supply/marketing system was a necessary (but not sufficient) condition of the mass equipping of the production units. However, the system broke down in the late 1970s and in the 1980s, when the economic environment deteriorated: the credit system no longer worked and the peasants' access to fertilizer was cut off.[12]

---

12. J.-M. Jung et al., *Le développement agricole du Sahel* [The Agricultural Development of the Sahel], Montpellier, CIRAD, 1993.

COMBINING TRADITIONAL AND MODERN TECHNOLOGIES

Considering the frequency of failure, requiring projects to be completely redesigned, and, conversely, the possibility of innovation under certain conditions, the questions that need to be asked are how one should manage the dissemination of technology having regard to the cultural dimensions linked to a specific ecosystem and how traditional skills and technologies can be combined with modern knowledge and know-how.

These are questions of capital importance in so far as history shows that a social group can assimilate a new technique only if it has already succeeded in mastering the previous techniques in the same branch of knowledge presupposed by the new technique. Innovation, the 'unknown', can arouse suspicion and mistrust. Only when its introduction is properly prepared, when it is to some degree of local origin, and when the risks are limited does it become easier to accept (see above).

In the medical field (pharmacopoeia and medicine proper) there have been increasing numbers of experiments with the adoption of traditional technologies, in particular in pharmacology, or with the combining of traditional and modern expertise, for example pairing witch-doctors or healers with psychiatrists in some African countries, notably Senegal.

Thus, although traditional folk medicine may appear fragile as compared with its scientific Western equivalent, often imported and imposed without discernment, many projects are aimed at recording tradition and reconciling it with modernity. In Central Africa, for instance, cells of traditional healers have been incorporated into modern medical teams in order to protect patients from the harmful effects of mixing traditional and modern prescriptions. Traditional practitioners in several regions have been trained in environmental health, preventive care, and nutrition and child care. Once trained, they join modern health-care teams. Similar steps have been taken to improve the training given to village birth attendants.

The same applies to agriculture and silviculture. Although subsistence agriculture is subject to ecological conditions of great diversity, it was long disdained by the experts. Recently, however, agronomists, having discovered that indigenous agriculture can form the basis for the scientific improvement of agricultural methods, have begun reviving the old practices. In fact, traditional agriculture incorporates a number of valuable, enduring principles: it uses few outside inputs, builds up the natural nutrients and efficiently recycles them, protects the soil (cover crops) and promotes genetic diversity.

The indigenous agro-forestry systems of the Sahel region, based on the acacia, are an example of the improved agricultural practices which could supplement fertilizer promotion projects in semi-arid countries. In Nigeria, traditional African itinerant farming practices have made it possible to develop a permanent cropping system called 'alley cropping'. Similarly, the revolt of the inhabitants of a village in southern Ghana, after two children had died of pesticide poisoning, led them to devise new agricultural techniques that reconcile traditional know-how (natural fertilizer, complementary cropping) with the principles of modern agriculture: new ploughing techniques have helped to control soil erosion and the leaching of nutrients by rain. It was found that, with a minimum of training on experimental farms, the peasants were perfectly able to master the new techniques and adapt intuitively to the principles of sustainable agriculture with modest input requirements.

The same observations could be made about handicrafts and small-scale commercial production. The maintenance of the structures and forms of traditional production, which can be reconciled with very modern forms of marketing at both the national and international level, enables the artistic quality of the products to be preserved, while maintaining traditional skills and family and social cohesion in its original cultural forms within a cottage industry context. With their potential for creating jobs and generating income in hard currencies, whose importance for countries with a balance of payments deficit needs no emphasizing, handicrafts and small-scale commercial production are considered by most developing countries as a form of cultural industry, from which much can be learned, particularly in connection with the search for a positive interaction between tradition, culture and development. The trading impact of the International Crafts Fair organized in Ouagadougou in October 1992, at which the crafts of Benin, Burkina Faso, Mali, Niger and Senegal were displayed, indicates that the culture/development interaction is favourable to this industry only when a wide selection of innovative quality products are shown and, above all, appropriate production and distribution structures are set up to meet demand outside Africa.[13]

Similarly, research work to define the role of crafts in development in Asia (India, Indonesia, Malaysia, Philippines, Sri Lanka and Thailand) shows that craft production is increasingly oriented towards exportation. This is leading to changes in the creative expression of crafts persons, and also presents the problem of the shift of activities from family workshops to factories where mechanization entails a huge loss of jobs for individual workers.[14]

The success of rural industries in the countries of South-East Asia, such as China and Thailand, testifies to this dynamic. The rural industries, often family concerns, but sometimes run by local communities, which have been able to win domestic and even international markets, have been built up on local artisanal traditions or to fill the gaps left by planning. They are solidly anchored in the cultural and social context of the countries concerned. Making optimum use of local potential, they demonstrate the population's creativity, technical skills and spirit of enterprise and innovation. These rural businesses now make up a by no means negligible part of the Chinese national economy, even though they only began to spring up in 1978. This use of local potential is also to be found in other fields, for example, the building of roads and other transport structures such as bridges. The superiority of local technical solutions in certain cases over what modern technology can offer is illustrated by the suspension bridges built in the Baglung district of Nepal. Local committees used their own technology to construct bridge piles of stone rather than concrete and to attach the bridge deck with locally made steel pins. Using steel cables supplied by the government they have built bridges with a span of up to 100 metres, taking two to three times less time than the Public Works Department and at one-eighth the cost, using manpower and techniques supplied exclusively by their own community.[15]

13. Africa Design International, *Bilan commercial du Salon international de l'artisanat* [Commercial Appraisal of the International Handicrafts Fair], Ouagadougou, 1992.
14. E. A. Pye, *Artisans in Economic Development: Evidence from Asia,* Ottawa, International Development Research Centre, 1980.
15. Cernea, op. cit., p. 383.

In conclusion, all these examples clearly show that drawing a sharp dividing line between innovation and modern technology, on the one hand, and local knowledge and know-how, on the other, does not enable a complete picture to be obtained of situations, problems and the possibilities of real solutions. It may even cause human and cultural resources available in a given population to be wasted. It is therefore essential that, not only in local development projects and programmes but also in those at national level, whether the initiative comes from outside or inside, an inventory of the skills available on the spot be drawn up, either for use as such or for combining with new techniques and skills, or else to serve as a basis for innovative experiments, in particular in certain priority areas of application.

CHAPTER 5

Development values: economic growth or human flowering?

Among the elements that go to make up a culture, as identified above, some may be considered strategic, since they determine the compatibility of development projects with local cultures and, more precisely, the acceptance or rejection by a given society of economic, social or technological change and the short- or medium-term sacrifices it implies.

Thus, it is essential to take these elements into account in order to ensure dialogue and participation, two indispensable conditions of success. They must therefore be defined in relation to the values that underlie development. This is why it is first necessary to explore the question of development and its ideology, in order that we may better understand what a development project means for the values, beliefs, customs and behaviour of a population.

Economism, economic growth and development

It is worth recalling the distinction made by the French economist François Perroux between economic growth and development.[1] Growth is a quantitative indicator applicable to the big items of the national accounts (per capita gross national product, gross domestic product, gross capital investment, etc.). Development, on the other hand, is bound up with economic, social and human progress, for man is both the engine and the ultimate goal of development.

1. F. Perroux, *A New Concept of Development*, Paris, UNESCO, 1983.

It must be the work of man who must also be its final purpose. But it has to be remembered that development is also a culture whose motivating values are belief in progress through science and the economy, a preference for modernity, the certainty of a better future, and wealth creation by accumulation of the profits made in economic activity. It must lastly be remembered that development is a long-term process that has to be planned in the short and medium term with very long-term goals in view.

Economists have always had human development through economic growth alone at the centre of their concerns. Even in the thinking of the physiocrats in the eighteenth century it is possible to discern the germ of the idea according to which society must be built and developed by setting individual happiness, achieved solely by economic means, as its ultimate goal. However, the rise of the commercial economy and capitalism thrust this humanist vision aside and put growth and short-term profit in its place.

In the second half of the twentieth century, recognition of the growing disparities in development prompted some co-operation organizations to take up once again the idea, inherited from the eighteenth century, of happiness through economic and technical progress. Thus, it was with a humanist intention that economic growth was chosen, as something self-evident, as the engine of development. At the same time, the strategy of certain big economic players continued to be based on the economicist option and the virtues of management, that is, the purely economic management of business in its most classic sense.

ECONOMICISM, THE ULTIMATE STAGE OF ECONOMISM

The principal feature of 'economicism' is the exclusive concern with maximizing the short-term profitability of every economic development project. It represents the most basic version of development with an economic 'engine'.

In reality, this approach corresponds to the culture of the industrial societies with a liberal economy based exclusively on the play of market forces and the predominance of entrepreneurial strategy. It implies strategic choices and motivating values similar to those of economically dominated development in general, but in a rather exacerbated form: hence the quest for competitiveness at any price, organization and efficiency, economic success measured in purely financial terms, and modernity as opposed to tradition, regarded as addiction to the past.

If one examines the general principles common to the economism and 'economicism' models of development, one finds that there are three:

1. *A linear and mechanical conception of history* which presupposes that all societies must necessarily pass through the same phases of development to reach the stage in which the economy is capable of providing the same level of prosperity as that enjoyed by the populations of the countries regarded as 'developed'. The perfect expression of this principle can be found in Rostow's famous theory, which distinguishes between five stages: traditional society (without science or technology), the pre-take-off stage (economic preliminaries, change of mentality), take-off (investment and savings, mass industrialization), maturity (adoption of modern technologies in every field) and, finally, the consumer society.

2. *An ethnocentric argument* which consists in considering that every society should adopt the values on which the Western societies are based: spirit of initiative, profit motive, competitiveness, the accumulation of wealth and material security.

3. *The assumptions of economism*, i.e. that the economy and hence the tools of economic policy are sufficient to enable a country to achieve its development goals.

This is a scheme of evolution which postulates that the road leading to development is unique, going in one direction and right for every country.[2] It must not be forgotten, however, that liberal thinking, on economic subjects as well as on others, includes the conviction that it is through economic freedom that the individual will best flourish and therefore attain happiness.

In cultural terms, this model is just as determinist and evolutionist: starting from an initial cultural situation, every culture must pass through a succession of historically necessary phases to reach the ultimate stage, that of modern – i.e. industrial, technical, rational, productivist and efficient – culture.

2. W. W. Rostow, *The Stages of Economic Growth*, New York, Cambridge University Press, 1962.

THE CULTURAL EFFECTS OF EXCLUSIVELY ECONOMIC DEVELOPMENT

The cultural and human effects of development with exclusively economic ends are well known: a consumer culture, excessive concentration of the population in the big cities, leading to uprooting and depersonalization, even dehumanization, and the destruction of nature and the environment. This situation poses a grave threat not only to individual societies but to the entire human species. Moreover, whatever the intentions of those who initiate them, operations which underestimate the cultural dimension, taking only the technical, economic and financial aspects into account, and apply models and techniques derived from the experience of the industrialized countries, cannot fully succeed, since they are unrealistic.

This is the nub of the difficulties encountered by the developing countries which achieved independence around the 1960s and have sought to build an autonomous economy. Even by the 1970s, the shortcomings of the strategies based on the need to 'catch up' on the 'advanced' countries and on ambitious plans for rapid mass industrialization (in particular, what have been called the 'industrializing industries') had become clear to all.

As has already been pointed out, this statement needs modifying to take into account the swift 'take-off' of some Asian countries. However, in their case, the principles of a Western-style economy have been reinterpreted by the peoples concerned, or rather their leaders, in terms of their own value systems and their 'economic culture' and have led them into accepting considerable sacrifices, if they feel that the effort will be borne by all, to achieve a certain improvement in their physical living conditions.

Moreover, as we have already seen, closer inspection leads to the conclusion that some countries are, as it were, 'half-way' to development and that, conversely, development and underdevelopment can coexist within the same country.

The problems of development, it should be noted, are not exclusive to the countries of the South. In the industrialized countries, the economic crisis which is shaking the world economy has brought crucial problems to light. Thus, the increased productivity and systematic mechanization that follow in areas such as agriculture have a harmful effect on the way of life of the peasant population, as on youth employment and the protection of the natural environment. Entire professions are condemned to die out completely, for example those connected with the sea and the exploitation of energy sources among others. Similarly, scientific and technical changes, especially in the fields of communications and information, present an impossible challenge to the systems of education that have been in operation until the present time. Moreover, the 'socialist' model, which seemed to represent an alternative to the mode of development of the 'capitalist' countries, has broken down in recent years. This means that in all the industrial societies the relevance of the dominant development models and their objectives is being increasingly questioned.

THE INTERFACE BETWEEN TRADITION AND MODERNITY

It is customary to draw a sharp dividing line between tradition and modernity. This makes it possible to understand the broad outlines of the conflicts that arise here and there between the various aspects of Western culture and the cultures of the non-European countries. However, it would be artificial to regard these cultures as being totally opposed. In reality, intercultural conflict is confined to certain very precise circumstances and the differences can be observed in certain everyday situations, in certain behaviour patterns and attitudes. Only if this reality is taken into account can one usefully explore the interface between tradition and modernity.

As we have seen, development confined to economicism inevitably involves two key concepts: economic growth as the engine and end purpose of development and maximum short-term profitability as the universal justification for action. These two concepts form the source of the cultural values identified above.

These are the values that may enter into conflict with those of the societies which still function essentially outside this model. In the industrialized countries, the values that make up the cultures of the past survive in weakened and more or less concealed form, but in the developing countries they still retain all their force.

Among the constituent elements of these cultures, some play a fundamental part, to the extent that they determine the world view and functional standards of the society and all its economic and social activities.

By and large, the interface between tradition and modernity

121

controls the compatibility of the cultural components of each. For the traditionalists, knowledge, know-how, values, forms, social and economic organization, behaviour models, and intellectual and artistic expression are enshrined, once and for all, in the corpus of tradition. Their validity depends on whether or not they conform to that tradition, whose pre-eminence derives from its very antiquity. Consequently, any change must be treated with the utmost caution and contemplated only to the extent that it does not formally conflict with this corpus.

The central position occupied by tradition in the interplay between culture and development cannot, however, be considered in purely negative terms. It is linked with the notion of the heritage, cultural identity and historical continuity of a society. It meets the need of every human community to see itself as the possessor of a rich heritage and as firmly rooted in its often mythical origins. Finally, the preservation of tradition plays a particularly important part in societies with a strong oral culture.

However, tradition cannot be understood as absolute and inflexible: it itself evolves. Indeed, every tradition is liable to reinterpretation in the course of the interplay between the various socioeconomic and cultural groups. The upholders of tradition may have an institutional basis for their role and thus exercise special power within society; for their part, the other groups or individuals may reinterpret tradition in terms of interests of a different nature and loosen its absolute grip. In this way, an apparently static society may develop more or less heterodox initiatives and innovations and make ultimately pluralistic advances.

In conclusion, it is the realization of the inadequacy, if not the outright failure, of purely economic development strategies, together with awareness of the human objectives of development, that has led to the very concept or content of the term development being re-examined from an entirely different point of view.

From this new viewpoint, development is seen as an evolutionary process involving a long-term, world-scale, 'holistic' approach to the future of society. To this extent, the human being is the origin, agent and ultimate purpose of development.[3]

3. See, in particular, UNESCO, *World Decade for Cultural Development: Plan of Action*, paras. 21–25, Paris, UNESCO, 1990. (UNESCO doc. CC-89/WS/20.)

Consequently, development includes economic growth, but at the same time it has many other dimensions and, indeed, serves to integrate all the dimensions of human activity, in particular the cultural dimension.

Finally, development is a mobilizing process, since it can only take place by marshalling all the energies of society, all of whose members must participate in the economic and social transformation of their community.

CHAPTER 6

Dynamics of the interactions between culture and development

Because of the number and complexity of the elements involved at the interface between culture and development, priority, in the methodological treatment proper, is given to the analysis of the positive and negative interactions between the above-mentioned cultural components or factors and the sectors of economic, technico-scientific and social activity.

However, this analysis is not confined to the interplay of reciprocal influences between different fields: it must also extend to the types of relations established within a given project between the various levels of intervention, from the initial decision to the implementation of the project and the evaluation of its effects. In a word, it is a matter of ranking the interacting players and factors.

Interaction between players and levels

Within a development policy or project, these interactions are the first important point needing to be examined for the purposes of this review. Here, it is a question of analysing the decision-making processes: how can one follow the process of decision-making, in particular starting from the evaluation of previous operations and the information and research relating to the problems involved, including the question of the context? How can one follow the progress of the initial idea or plan, from the standpoint of both strategy and content? What distortions does it undergo? Above all, how are the strategy, policy and project interpreted in the field?

This requires our interaction analysis to be focused, initially, on the interaction between the decision-makers at the apex of the decision 'pyramid' and then on the 'downstream' phase leading from decision to implementation, on the relations between the local and non-local players, and finally on the upstream phase: in what form and in accordance with what selection criteria (that is, in the form of untargeted information or specific assessment) does data flow back from the 'field' to the top of the 'pyramid', so that it can be decided whether the action should be continued, corrected or replaced by other forms of intervention?

Finally, mention must be made of the beneficiary population's participation in the project, from planning to implementation and evaluation. In itself, participation is the best and perhaps the only way of taking the cultural dimension of development into account. Its effective realization poses complex problems and justifies a pedagogical approach, which should include sharpening awareness among the decision-makers and training development workers, as well as keeping the general public informed.

In short, it is clear that the analysis of the interaction between culture and development brings into play a number of complex but significant elements capable of providing solutions to the problems of how to incorporate cultural factors and effects in development.

In fact, analysing these interactions at the methodological level itself will make it possible to move on to systems analysis aimed at providing an understanding of the global functioning of all the various factors and effects involved in the development process and, consequently, will assist with the design of integrated development policies and projects. Finally, it will ensure that cultural factors and problems can be given their proper place in the devising and evaluation of international strategies, in particular the United Nations Development Strategy for the Nineties and the following decades.

Lastly, the interactions at work between the various levels of decision and action must feature in any experiments in globalizing the interactions to be taken into account in analysing development processes, as will be seen in Part Three of this review.

Interaction between the various factors

The first point here concerns the de facto interaction, firstly between structuring and structured cultural factors and secondly between cultural and non-cultural factors. It is clear, for example, that such a relationship exists between beliefs and traditions and certain dietary habits, certain norms that govern family life, and indeed the models of production and economic activity, even if in this latter case powerful opposing influences may be at work.

As we know, cultural factors may have both positive and negative effects on the various forms of economic and social life. In particular, the question of cultural 'roadblocks' calls for closer examination. Very often the latter are only viewed as such by the developers because their preliminary analysis of the situation was faulty and/or because they adopted a short-term approach.

Much more important is the question of the cultural dynamics of development, which may have their origin in the motivating values present in the culture of the population concerned. Even the feeling of cultural identity, which may sometimes have destructive side-effects, can be the engine of a community's economic and social transformation. Some people call this having confidence in one's own culture.

Conversely, measures taken in the economic or social fields must necessarily interact with the local sociocultural context. Some aspects of these measures could have a traumatizing effect on the existing behaviour models and modes of life, whereas careful preparation would help to make them much more acceptable to the population.

Raising the question of the possibly negative cultural effects of development opens up the wider problem of the cultural impact of development, the evaluation of which is one of the means of taking the cultural factors into account in development projects by measuring their positive and negative effects – which means that the instruments needed for the purpose have to be available.

This question also raises the problem of the interaction between local culture and external cultural inputs. Economic growth, the increasing complexity of the division of labour, goods, services and trade and the diversification of institutions and organizations are the visible and tangible manifestations of a way of life interiorized by the individual members of society through and in their culture.

However, these interactions inevitably introduce an outside cultural content into the pre-existing one. Today, no society is culturally self-sufficient and the phenomenon has been considerably accelerated by the lightning advances in means of transport, communications and the media.

Furthermore, acculturation, a form of intercultural relations, cannot be regarded as an exclusively negative effect of development, given the increasing internationalization of the world, provided that it implies not the rejection of one's own culture but its gradual unfolding – of which history provides so many examples.

Cultural impact of development

As we have just seen, the question of the cultural impact of development is closely linked with the problem of interaction. The term itself suggests culture shock and thus raises the question of 'zones' of incompatibility and, secondarily, that of the pace of the process of change at work in society.

As pointed out above, outside economic, technical and organizational inputs inevitably introduce different cultural contents, an effect intensified by the very rapid advances being made in transport, communications and the media. This situation is not in itself intrinsically harmful. The history of the world is studded with contacts between different societies and the resulting symbioses have been far from wholly negative.

The transformations may affect areas considered essential by the local population; changes apparently confined to the economy or social and organizational reform may result in extensive cultural destabilization, with the population either adopting an attitude of rejection or losing confidence in its own ability to adapt the changes to its needs, mentality and way of life and, consequently, losing confidence in the national authorities since they appear to be the authors of these rapid changes – or at least partners in them.

This may be the case, for example, when traditional food crops and agricultural techniques are replaced by the techniques of modern agronomy and mechanized farming, when the system of land-ownership is modified, when custom is replaced by written law, when changes are made in the manner of organizing time – the day, seasons and agrarian cycles, and the alternation of work and rest –

and, finally, when modern medical practices are substituted for local medicines and the work of healers and witch-doctors.

The problem here is the rapidity, indeed violence, and extent of the changes, which are often imposed. Thus, the uncontrolled development of mass tourism can result in the disappearance of other occupations and local cultural values and behaviour.[1] The rapid modernization of agriculture speeds up rural migration to the cities with the consequent uprooting and marginalization of the new migrants, especially women, and periods of sometimes very difficult adaptation for those who migrate from the countries of the South to the industrialized countries.

Thus, the risks of sociocultural destabilization which may arise in these situations need to be contained and the cultural adaptation of the population facilitated by providing for participation and appropriate educational support.

In other words, it is a question of determining the conditions on which pre-existing cultural configurations can be modified by introducing new activities and strategies without undermining people's cultures or weakening their confidence in those cultures or, even better, while making their culture the basis or indeed the accelerator of development.

If no such precautions are taken, the customs and modes of thought of the population will act as brakes on over-rapid and over-extensive change (for example, in the areas of school attendance and birth control). Measuring the cultural impact of development makes it possible to assess the acceptability of innovation and outside inputs and the stresses or even conflicts which their sudden introduction might provoke. Conversely, the preferences of the population confronted by innovation will need to be identified by the methods to be described in the later chapters of this document.

But clearly the detail in which these cultural configurations can be taken into account will vary with the level of decision, for example, between large-scale development policies and programmes and grass-roots projects. At the macro level, taking account of cultural data in major policy directions and conditions for implementation in project planning and execution will be in the form of major

1. UNESCO, *Proceedings of the Seminar on the Incorporation of the Cultural Dimension into a Project for Integrated Local Development in Tunisia*, Paris, UNESCO, 1988. (UNESCO doc. CC/CSP/FCP/10.)

objectives and recurrent cultural characteristics (regularities). Conversely, in the case of field projects the specific cultural features of a given place or area can be considered in greater detail. Another solution would be to employ a so far little-used technique for project formulation, namely project 'clusters' comprising a number of small projects connected with general policy definitions laid down in large-scale outline projects. UNDP, for example, is beginning to change over from the planning of individual projects to an approach by programme.

Thus the dynamics of the interactions between culture and development, which enables the internal components of culture and the meeting-points between culture and development to be understood, opens up a path towards the 'modelization' of integrated development (see Part Three). In a different form and by a different scientific approach we will have arrived at the same conclusions as Robert Klitgaard, who proposed, at an international conference, three equations crystallizing the importance of culture: its main features and factors, ranging from the most general to the most concrete (utilities), its influence on development choices and paths and, thirdly, the transformations that all cultures undergo because of economic and social change.[2]

2. R. Klitgaard, 'Taking Culture into Account: From "Let's" to "How" ', in *Culture and Development in Africa* (conference proceedings), Vol. I, pp. 86–7, Washington, D.C., World Bank, 1992.

CHAPTER 7

Priority areas of application and new strategies

So far, we have used a simple model to classify development strategies and projects into one of two categories: economic development or social development. Our intention now is to review the problems which arise when allowance is made for cultural factors and effects in the concrete action pursued in the economic and social spheres, that is, at the level of practical implementation and in the situations which have been recognized as meriting priority. A series of new propositions will therefore be put forward in the following pages.

In the economic sphere, emphasis will accordingly be placed on the following aspects: savings, enterprise, the informal sector, and crop and animal farming. In the social sphere, the main attention will focus on basic education, health action, food/nutrition, habitat, accommodation and urban development, the family and, last but not least, the role of women in development.

In all these activities, traditional patterns and norms of behaviour still play an important and dynamic role. This precludes their outright replacement by modern regulatory models and procedures without first ascertaining whether they can coexist and be combined, or even assessing whether it would not be preferable to build on the existing foundation, with such improvements and consolidation as may be necessary.

Economic areas

SAVINGS STRATEGIES

As we have seen previously, attempts to collect and mobilize savings in the modern banking system have more often than not turned out to be inappropriate. In parallel, traditional systems for collecting funds and lending which suit the way of life and thought patterns of the local population continue to prosper and give appreciable service, particularly in the informal sector and for small businesses. This is the case in particular in some countries of Africa or Asia, or in the diasporas originating from those two continents which still use the old ways of saving and borrowing, even in a modern economy (cf. reference to tontines on p. 107 above).

Bankers and financial experts must therefore adapt and improve their methods. The traditional ways of collecting funds must also be consolidated and enhanced so as to mobilize 'sleeping' savings or retain locally resources which tend to be expatriated. Above all, the aspirations, sensitivities and motivations of the populations concerned must be respected. For example, the Grameen Bank founded in Bangladesh in 1969 shows how a loan system can be developed for the very poor. Its creator, Mohammad Yunus, takes as his starting-point the fact that landless farmers have no access to credit simply because they have no collateral to offer. However, he goes on to show that, contrary to received wisdom, the poorest are not necessarily the worst payers. The 'bank', which only attained this status in 1983, began on a modest scale with its founder's own money and the help of his students. The form chosen was the joint loan.

Applicants for loans, all from the most disadvantaged rural milieux, first had to form a group of five borrowers. Meeting regularly with a clerk working at the bank, they learned the basic principles. To begin with only two were allowed to borrow. The others were only given loans once the first paid back interest and capital by instalments spread over fifty weeks. This meant that the collateral requirement could be dispensed with. Loans can now be granted for various economic activities at the borrower's choice but they have to be economically viable: cycle rickshaws, dairy cows, weaving, pottery and repair shops.

The projects financed are not sufficient for the area's real economic take-off but the beneficiaries of the Grameen Bank's loans

have a 20 per cent better standard of living than other landless peasants. It has begun to develop broader and more traditional economic activities, such as irrigation projects, and has grown from
about 100 branches in 1984 to 500 in 1988 with 500,000 custom-
ers. In a country where they are the most disadvantaged, 80 per
cent of loans go to women. The bank loan repayment rate is 98 per
cent: 'A banker's dream,' says Mohammad Yunus with a smile.[1]

This example shows that the scale of the operations to be conducted is of course an important factor. For the informal sector, as
will later be seen, small-scale saving and small businesses sometimes
constitute a 'fabric' that is favourable to the emergence of an endogenous development dynamic. The same consideration would not,
for example, apply to major industrial operations. Experience, too,
has proved that such complex projects are not necessarily adapted
to the sociocultural context of some parts of the world. On the other
hand, in regions such as East Asia, major operations may be combined with activities on a smaller scale but structured round the
large actions.

BUSINESS AND CULTURE

A company may be defined as a body which brings together functions and economic and social actors with a view to the production
or distribution of goods and services. Its legal status (public or private), and national or international affiliations, naturally generate a
number of important cultural consequences. A public corporation is
expected to place greater emphasis on the idea of public service. An
international corporation is bound to embody the culture of its origins. A company also brings together two categories of decision-
makers at very different levels, employers and employees, whose
goals and interests will not necessarily be identical and may even be
diametrically opposed.

This is where the concept of the corporate spirit comes into
play for the employer, as the embodiment of the professional quality
of his company, while the employees, for their part, are confronted
with the interplay of three cultures: their own, that of the employer
and the corporate culture which he will endeavour to promote.

1. UNESCO, *Meeting of Experts on the Cultural Dimension of Development,*
   para. 55, Paris, UNESCO, 1991. (Working document.)

Because of these factors, social aspirations are bound to take second place to economic goals in any corporate strategy.

However, regardless of the type of company involved, the nature of its activities will always require a rational form of organization, particularly in respect of the work of its employees. Work in itself is a cultural reality whose importance is decisive. Depending on its content (creative or repetitive), its duration measured in hours per day or week, and the position assigned to the employee in the hierarchy of giving and carrying out instructions, its significance for the employee will differ completely – ranging from alienation to participation in a collective endeavour. Moreover, the 'corporate culture' will take a different form depending on whether the business strategy is defined and put in place by the public authorities or a private entrepreneur, and by national or foreign decision-makers. The size of the business will also have a direct bearing on the nature of the human relations between its different categories of personnel.

This is where the specific culture of the employees of a company comes into play, that is, their professional experience and expertise, their physical and intellectual aptitudes, and above all their ways of thinking and their lifestyle. These factors will inevitably affect assiduity, the desire to perform well and the ability to become integrated into a specific hierarchical structure. This in turn may affect the ease of adaptation to the pace of activity imposed by the requirements of production, organizational norms, the search for maximum efficiency and the time which elapses between the performance of an activity and the reward for it. Family or ethnic ties may interfere with the hierarchical relationships, above all if a conflict arises between the company and its employees.

However, as is the case in some Asian countries, a basic consensus can be established, for a certain time at least, between the employees and the economic or policy decision-makers who are responsible for defining and developing the corporate strategy with a view to the optimization of growth, at least if their competence in this regard is not disputed. But it is hardly likely that this corporate culture will be furthered and genuinely accepted by the employees if it conflicts with their own values, motivations and centres of interest.[2]

2. S. H. K. Yeh, *Understanding Development: Modernization and Cultural Values in Asia and the Pacific Region*, Paris, UNESCO, 1989. (UNESCO doc. STY.89.)

THE INFORMAL SECTOR

The informal sector of the economy consists of a number of production and trading structures and activities which may be characterized by their size (small businesses), the continuity (or discontinuity) of their activities, the low level of their investments in plant (and hence of the risks incurred) and their small number of staff.

Conventional economic analysis would probably not consider the performance of these activities and structures to be adequate. On the other hand, a cultural approach will enable the importance of cultural factors in this area to be highlighted: firstly, the presence and use of local knowledge and expertise which may be unofficial but are nevertheless operational in their own way; secondly, a function of responding to the needs of the population, either to satisfy a particular type of demand for goods and services for everyday use at a modest price, or else to absorb into the urban environment some members of the floating and unemployed population who will thus be enabled to survive.

The legal status of businesses of this kind may vary widely: official existence, tolerated activities, marginal or even illicit trading. Examples include family workshops in certain craft specializations, the 'little trades', street vendors, mobile tradesmen, 'moonlighting', the black market and smuggling.

These activities are the result of either individual initiatives taken in the 'gaps' which remain in institutionalized economic life or else a form of creative response to the weaknesses and deficiencies of the official economic system. They are also bound up with the very high rate of unemployment in many countries of the world and the need for people to find jobs of whatever kind. These are often precarious and badly paid, but can nevertheless provide the resources necessary to live, or at least to survive, especially in the big urban centres – even for young adults who have completed their secondary or higher education but cannot enter the job market.

However, these considerations must not lead to the mistaken conclusion that some of these activities, in particular those which take the form of small businesses, have no real prospect of lasting and developing further; some may even grow into small businesses which are capable of pursuing their own independent development or of becoming subcontractors to larger companies.

Can the activities of the informal sector, especially in the shape of small businesses, be seen as the components of a spontaneous economic fabric reflecting the dynamism and creativity of population groups whose abilities might gradually be channelled towards businesses organized on more modern lines? The foregoing comments on activities of this kind show that no general answer can be given to this question.

However, it would certainly be useful to study the evolution of small businesses in the countries of East Asia, or among the Asian communities in Western countries, where many initiatives of this kind have sprung up since the 1980s. But these initiatives have grown out of a special context in which a strong bond exists between the spheres of culture and the economy and where common cultural traits are clearly apparent, despite the diversity of the prevailing situations.

CROP AND ANIMAL FARMING

The importance of cultural factors in dietary habits, including prohibitions (see below), is also reflected in the practices of crop and animal farming. A great many factors come into play here: the status of land-ownership under customary or modern law, individual or collective ownership of the land and farm holdings, presence of a population of farm workers with a precarious status and the type of farming that is practised (subsistence or cash-crop production) and the techniques employed – 'slash and burn', crop rotation, use of natural (including human) or chemical fertilizers, seasonal activity patterns and land irrigation practices.

All these factors condition both the economic configuration and the cultural significance of agriculture. For example, if subsistence agriculture is replaced by cash-crop farming for local or export sales, the cultural universe of the local population is liable to be seriously disturbed. Agronomists must always bear these realities in mind when they begin to apply their knowledge and expertise to a human environment with which they are unfamiliar. In this respect, the creation of participative structures and voluntary local co-operative movements can play an essential role.

Similarly, in the animal farming sector, allowance must be made for the economic and symbolic, or even religious, status of the animals that are part of the everyday world of rural people. The consequences which flow from this have a decisive bearing on the exploitation of food resources (milk, meat), other products (hides), or the physical strength which animals can provide. In some agro-pastoral societies of the Sahel countries or of East Africa, the size of the herd of cattle is far more a symbol of social prestige than a purely economic asset.

The type of animal farming – extensive or intensive – is another important aspect. If cattle-raising is extensive, the population will be nomadic rather than sedentary. We know the extent to which this factor conditions the culture of populations of this kind. We are also familiar with the cultural trauma which may result from the enforced sedentarization of nomadic populations. At the same time, this phenomenon poses difficult development problems. Finally, allowance must be made for the fact that certain nomadic populations, or peoples with a tribal form of social organization, are determined to remain outside the rules of the sedentary, and a fortiori the modern, world.

Social issues

EDUCATION

The fundamental role of education in development strategies, at the level of both international programmes and national policies, seems more or less self-evident. In addition, political leaders and senior civil servants consider the role of the scientific and technical disciplines in this educational process to have a decisive bearing on the economic and intellectual progress of any society.

However, a number of distinctions must be drawn here, in regard both to the content of education and to the population groups which are to be educated. Identical programmes cannot be offered to schoolchildren and students, let alone adults, drawn from different cultural backgrounds: that fact seems to be generally recognized and self-evident. But much still remains to be done before it is put into effect in the revision of curricula and teaching methods for education both in and out of school.

In the area of basic education (literacy training, health and family education, acquisition of new skills, especially in the rural environment), all programmes which are connected with the cultural environment of the population for whom these programmes are designed avoid the difficulties and risk of rejection that may be encountered with the local population in some cases. On the contrary, this type of programme motivates them strongly to take advantage of basic education activities.

Cases are met, however, of certain populations rejecting the forms of education offered them, and this reaction is partly cultural in origin: they find no reflection of their own culture, aspirations and way of life, which would justify such education in their eyes. Moreover, the content, teaching methods and institutional framework of schooling necessarily call into question traditional forms of education, that is, the education of young people by their elders in certain societies or education-initiation based on religious practices.

This brief review raises the issue of the cultural causes and effects of the crisis in education which can be observed all over the world today: quite apart from the inadequacy of the resources deployed, for example for literacy training, existing systems do not respond to these qualitative needs and are not adapted to the economic, social and cultural situation of the population, in particular of young people. In the urban environment especially, existing systems are spurned or rejected by the very persons who are in the greatest need of suitable education to improve their living conditions and later facilitate their entry into active life.

Another reason for this partial rejection of education by the populations concerned, especially young people, lies in the scale and rapidity of political, economic and cultural change in every society. The effects of this evolution, amplified by the media, may give young people the impression that all lasting values and references have been abolished and that all events are of equal significance (or insignificance).

The expansion of the young population, especially in the countries of the South, and the continuing advance of scientific and technical knowledge which has acquired the status of a body of 'super-knowledge', together with living conditions in the urban environment, may seriously weaken family and social structures and often result in cultural models that are purely materialistic. All of these trends pose immediate problems to educators and the persons responsible for educational policy. At the same time they call for long-term action, reflecting an approach which is at one and the same time educational and cultural.

ACTION ON HEALTH

The status of health and sickness differs from one culture to another, as therefore do the ways of treating and curing illnesses and
the medicines that are used. We shall confine ourselves here to a
reference to the role of traditional medicines, in particular medica-
tion by plants whose virtues are known to some custodians of traditional knowledge, for example, the medicine men and sorcerers of
Africa or the shamans in Asia and Latin America whose functions
include those of healers (see below).

The importance attached by the local people to this type of
medicine is such that careful attention must be given to the procedures and pace with which modern medicine is introduced into a
different cultural universe. In some cases, the combined use of traditional and modern medicine might be envisaged. This approach
seems to have given appreciable results not only in the treatment of
certain common illnesses, but also in psychiatric medicine and in
the treatment of psychosomatic disorders in which doctors and
healers are sometimes teamed up together. To take an example, the
vaccination campaign that was part of the efforts made in the 1960s
by WHO and USAID covering the whole of the African continent
with the object of eliminating smallpox met with particular resistance in the Yoruba-speaking areas of Nigeria and Benin. According
to Yoruba tradition, smallpox is the punishment for an offence
against Zakpata, god of the land, and may only be treated by the
relevant expiatory rites performed by healers. For this reason very
few people living in the Yoruba villages came forward to be vacci-
nated when the mobile medical teams came to their locality. It was
only when the international team discovered the origin of the problem and secured the assistance of the healers that the villagers began
to attend in large numbers. This example shows that values and
beliefs are not unalterable. If they are given the right kind of opportunity to weigh up the advantages of new practices, the villagers
generally tend to act in the direction of their own interests, without
necessarily giving up their old beliefs.[3]

3. D. Gentil, *Épargne, crédit et financement* [Saving, Credit and Financ-
    ing], Paris, Université de Paris X, 1991–92. (DESS course paper.)

Another aspect of health education resides in the use of local means of cultural expression to put across the fundamentals of health education in hygiene, for example, the need to avoid the consumption of polluted water. A good example is the work done among women in some rural parts of India by a specialized NGO (Asian Centre for Organization, Research and Development).[4]

This experience also poses the problem of the correct identification of the target population so as to gain cultural acceptance and effective participation in the actions which are conducted: in 1985, UNICEF recognized that, in cultural terms, mothers were the most appropriate discussion partner on measures for the benefit of African children. Similarly, birth-control programmes must first win over the support of husbands and mothers-in-law of married women (see Kenya case-study on pages 101–2).

But cultural factors and effects are still more crucial in dealing with pandemics like AIDS and scourges such as the growing abuse of drugs all over the world.

In the case of drugs, the factors which tend to encourage abuse, particularly by young people, are essentially of a sociocultural order: the pseudo-community aspect of consumption, curiosity about prohibited forms of behaviour, inadequate education, isolation associated with the deterioration of social structures, urban development and unemployment. Similarly, the use of drugs results in a subculture of withdrawal from the struggle for daily life and the drowning of one's difficulties as well as becoming a member of a supposed élite that is able to indulge in the luxury of transgressing general social rules, so creating a 'cult of exclusion'.

The cultural factors and effects of the spread of AIDS should perhaps also be investigated on the same lines, and are in any case linked in part with the continuing growth of drug abuse. But the transmission of the illness chiefly by sexual contact is also largely dependent on the habits, practices and value systems of the partners concerned, especially men, and on their sense of responsibility in relations with their sexual partners. Preventive education programmes against AIDS have also been seriously impeded by cultural taboos, for example, the refusal to discuss sexual problems

4. Asian Centre for Organization, Research and Development (ACORD), *Programmes and Activities,* New Delhi, ACORD, 1989.

explicitly in public, and by official denials due to the fear of 'losing face' by comparison with other countries. For instance, the ARCA (Religious Anti-AIDS Support) project mounted in Brazil on the initiative of ISER (Instituto de Estudios Religiosos) tackles the AIDS problem from the viewpoint of the various religious (mainly Candomblé, Catholic and Protestant) backgrounds in the country. Because of the need to be fully informed from the inside of the systems of representation and beliefs and practices connected with the Afro-Brazilian cults and to work in close collaboration with those best able to reinterpret them and steer them in the direction of preventive action against the virus, Candomblé priests and priestesses have been closely involved in the educational and re-socialization actions organized in this field, thus ensuring a broader and more effective dissemination of information among the people.[5]

FOOD AND NUTRITION

Food habits constitute one of the behaviour patterns whose cultural substrate is most apparent. They are also one of those aspects of a society's lifestyle in which economic, technical and social changes are reflected by profound and rapid cultural changes causing, in their turn, other economic, social and political changes. The changes in certain food habits may, in some cases, be considerable and happen swiftly, but there are other deeply rooted food customs which reappear at certain important occasions in life and which, for reasons that are partly religious and partly due to the almost immemorial appreciation or depreciation of certain products, may be regarded as permanent cultural features.

Examples of food habits modelled on cultural norms or values are numerous. They may have a religious basis, correspond to differentiations in social behaviour or serve to signal important moments in the year or in family or community life. The motivations may also overlap, thus strengthening or weakening the behaviour patterns that stem from them. They are, in any event, powerful cultural 'markers': vegetarian or meat diets, appreciation

---

5. See H. Panhuys, E. Sizoo and T. Verhelst, *La prise en compte des facteurs culturels dans les projets de développement* [Taking Cultural Factors into Account in Development Programmes], Part 1, para. I.1, Paris, UNESCO, 1993. (UNESCO doc. CLT-93/WS/3.)

or depreciation – or even rejection – of certain foodstuffs, organization or ad hoc nature of the act of eating.

This general statement needs also to be conditioned by three recent developments that overturn the previous equilibria. First there is the change in agricultural production methods in the broad sense: crop and animal farming, fishing, changes in food as a source of cultural models and the accentuation in certain areas of the world of the imbalances between quantitative and qualitative food requirements and the production/distribution of food products to meet these requirements whilst also meeting real nutritional needs.

A second point is the complete break between lifestyles and food production, whence arises the lack of nutrition or undernourishment found all too often in certain parts of the world. The reference here is to extreme cases where urgent action has to be taken and which are bound up with international or internal (refugees) emergencies or with certain ethnic or socio-economic groups (nomadic peoples, tribal groups, ethnic minorities, marginalized social categories). But the solution to these situations is not simply humanitarian. It is also a matter of making good, as far as possible, the cultural traumas these people have been through, using cultural as well as other means – in other words helping them to recover their own living models, but taking corrective action also, where that seems necessary (food habits for children, for example), while respecting the internal rationality of these people's food customs.

Lastly, the change in food models, which in certain of its aspects is one of the manifestations of globalization and modernity at work in every field, is also – for some economically or socially advantaged groups or certain age-groups in the industrialized countries – a way of setting oneself apart from the common practice in order to assert one's cultural or social specificity as compared with the rest of the community (dominant position or rejection of the cultural consensus on which the cohesion of the community is based). But what may appear to be 'deculturation' may also be one of the indicators of the challenging of what is or has been described by the holders of traditional power in all fields as an 'untouchable' cultural tradition, referring, in fact, to an 'untouchable' social tradition.[6]

6. See D. Desjeux, *Le sens de l'autre* [Awareness of Others], pp. 121–31, Paris, UNESCO/ICA, 1991.

HOUSING, ACCOMMODATION AND URBAN
DEVELOPMENT

From time immemorial and in all societies, the type of living environment – its internal organization for purely functional purposes or with a symbolic significance and its relationship with the outside world – has been one of the most telling ways in which individual cultures, their value systems, ways of life and social organization are expressed.

The rapid growth of the urban population and the need, at least in principle, to provide accommodation for it have resulted in a radical change in building techniques and models. Social housing policies have taken the place of the strategies and housing previously developed and built by the people themselves. Forms of urban development have thus been encouraged which result at one and the same time in the loss of identity of the inhabitants, a deterioration in living conditions through the provision of limited spaces which are standardized by uniform planning models, and urban segregation as the natural outcome of the social or cultural segregation suffered by certain social groups or communities because they belong to different cultures. What is more, urban development itself very often follows the dictates of profitability (price of land) and road traffic constraints. Finally, the imported architectural models and the building techniques employed are very often unsuitable for the climatic conditions prevailing in the countries concerned.

Here a whole range of cultural factors comes into play. The new arrivals must of course find accommodation. But the techniques of the mass housing which is provided, often in the form of high-rise apartment blocks, prevent the migrant populations from retaining their previous way of life, conviviality and family relationships. They therefore experience difficulties of adaptation which may take the form of a cultural trauma leading to dangerous forms of behaviour and marginal situations. The quality of housing may prove yet another cultural shock to peoples who are projected into an urban world with which they are more often than not unfamiliar, except through rejection or by the fragile and hazardous channels of the informal sector (small businesses, odd jobs, temporary work, moonlighting, and even illegal activities such as peddling, smuggling, etc.). Finally, the populations more often than not experience a profound malaise in the face of the types of housing which are imposed

143

on them. To take an example, the planners in a Middle Eastern country entrusted the construction of a town for 20,000 inhabitants to a group of consulting engineers consisting of both foreign and local experts. The town was to accommodate nomads who were rather favourably inclined to a certain form of sedentarization. The town plan was designed on 'chequerboard' lines, with streets intersecting each other at right angles. Each house had two rooms of the same size with a kitchen behind. Despite intensive efforts, the failure of this project was spectacular. The town was built, but remained unoccupied: the nomads used their own resources to build another residential zone with a semi-circular layout and the house of the chief in the centre. Each little house had two rooms of unequal size to which access was gained via the kitchen. A brief study in the field revealed the reasons for this failure: the nomads' tents were traditionally divided into two compartments of different size, the smaller being allocated to the women and the larger to the men, so respecting the rules of sexual segregation inherent in the social and cultural structure of the tribe. Before entering the tents, they used to greet the fire which was laid at the main entrance. In the new buildings, the nomads had replaced the eternal fire of their former home by the kitchen which contained the cooking hearth.[7]

However, many creative initiatives have been taken in this area. They deserve to be observed and supported as manifestations of a cultural dynamic and as an active response to the problems of urban life.

Although it may be paradoxical to consider the creation of precarious forms of habitat (e.g. shanty towns) as a first aspect of this cultural dynamic, the restoration of cultural and social ties between the members of a single community scattered over the great megacities of the South or of the industrialized countries is still more significant. These new groupings may result in the search for solutions by town planners and social agencies to equip the underprivileged districts with public services that are often lacking, to rehabilitate urban areas which are deteriorating, or even to contribute to the survival of old centres that are threatened with disappearance. For example, in the development of a settlement on the periphery of

---

7. D. Benham, *Culture et développement en Afrique du Nord et au Moyen-Orient* [Culture and Development in North Africa and the Middle East], pp. 24–6, Paris, UNESCO, 1992. (UNESCO doc. SHS.93/WS/4.)

Guadalajara (Mexico), the following phenomena were observed. First of all it has to be pointed out that the urban development described is quite illegal. Each dwelling is built more or less exclusively by the restricted or enlarged family unit. It is only later that the new arrival appeals to his neighbours, thus constituting small groups that are useful for solving problems concerning the group as a whole. The life of these groups is temporary. Within this general picture behaviour varies with the persons concerned. Those that are most dynamic tend to look outwards, seeking solutions to common problems in a concerted manner. The others take a more individual approach. To start with, people are primarily concerned with defending the land they occupy, but as more dwellings are built, new requirements arise (water, electricity, etc.). Then the most dynamic people extend their activities towards the public sector and seek institutional recognition by the authorities. This is the first step along the road towards the creation of an internal organization. Bit by bit, links are forged with the official organizations and what was initially an informal organization has now become institutionalized.[8]

THE ROLE OF WOMEN IN DEVELOPMENT

One of the groups of indicators of human development laid down by UNDP for the developing countries relates to the disparity between men and women on a number of points: percentage of the population, life expectancy, literacy, average number of years of study, attendance in primary, secondary and higher education, employment and responsibilities in public life. On the other hand, the rate of employment is the only criterion referred to when defining the situation of women in the industrialized countries. All the other conditions for the participation of women in the development of the industrialized countries would seem to have been satisfied. But their participation remains variable – and on the whole unsatisfactory – in the developing countries.

To obtain a more complete picture of the situation, having due

8. G. Solinis, *Organisation, dynamique culturelle et participation dans l'aménagement d'un quartier périphérique (Guadalajara, Mexico)* [Organization, Cultural Dynamics and Participation in the Development of a Periurban Area (Guadalajara, Mexico)], Paris, UNESCO, 1989. (UNESCO doc. CC/CSP/CD/03.)

regard to the diversity of the cultural contexts, it seems preferable to approach the problem from a different angle: that of the distribution of family and social duties between men and women in a great many societies. The present situation is of course undergoing far-reaching changes.

The whole complex of sociocultural values in respect of family life, continuity between the generations and the educational role of mothers underlies the features which, taken together, define the situation of women in society. But in some societies the rules of behaviour are often dictated by husbands, by the brothers of young unmarried women or by mothers-in-law. Although the authority of women is restricted for a part of their lives, they gain influence as they grow older and become the supreme arbiters of certain problems or conflicts which arise in the household.

One of the decisive criteria relating to the attainment of independence by women concerns the opportunities open to them to follow normal schooling and perhaps take up employment afterwards. A second is their ability to choose the number of children that they will bear. These two problems are in fact linked, since young women are very often prevented from pursuing a normal course of study by marriage and early motherhood.

However, this does not imply that women who have not followed a lengthy course of study are destined for the sole role of motherhood. In Africa, for example, many women engage in trade or craft activities. Moreover, within the family itself, women are able to exert their influence or take discrete and tenacious action designed to guide the choices which seem at first sight to be made entirely by the family system in its conventional form.

The cultural impact of development can also be observed in the evolution of the general status of women. This is partly the outcome of action by specialized movements and international organizations; but the economic and political transformations which are taking place all over the world and bringing women new responsibilities are a still more important factor.

A significant evolution of the status of women in some countries of North Africa and the Middle East can thus be observed in the wake of economic development and changes in political life. The spread of schooling, access for women to the employment market and new models of consumption have changed traditional attitudes. Admittedly, women still do not remain permanently single and men

146

continue to marry late. But the phenomenon of repudiation is on the wane and the essential adjustment of manpower is made by raising the age at which girls marry for the first time: the decline in early marriage is so pronounced that the number of single women at the age of 20 has doubled in the past fifteen years in Tunisia and Kuwait and even quadrupled in Algeria, where the phenomenon is connected with the acute housing shortage. A similar situation, albeit in a quite different context, applies in China.[9]

All in all, an analysis of the many situations in which women make a decisive contribution to cultural, social, political, and even economic change in their community demonstrates that the obstacles to the attainment by women of full rights are not insurmountable. On the contrary, a number of important changes are under way: while the rules of traditional marriage, based on the young age of the future bride and the size of her dowry, continue to be widely practised in some countries, especially in Africa, South Asia and the Islamic nations, the political and economic evolution of the world is leading an ever-increasing number of women to take on responsibilities in public life, for example in India or in the countries where a struggle for national freedom is in progress. The transformation of the general conditions of everyday life in many societies is also inducing women to have fewer children. But let us make no mistake about it: in some cases, traditional cultural factors are still a powerful brake on this evolutionary process. An example of this is the fact that, in production units or work shifts in Madagascar, the technological roles are allotted on the basis of sex or age criteria and individuals change job as they change their age-group. The division of labour by sex, the foundation of society here, is not a simple technological arrangement. Apart from the fact that the distribution of jobs does not always fit in with the 'natural skills' of each sex, this production relationship is co-ordinated with other forms of employment relations. The division of labour and chain of authority correspond to a hierarchy of status, each status being determined by the conditions of community reproduction and codified by family relationships.[10]

9. D. Benham, *Culture, démographie et développement* [Culture, Population and Development], Paris, UNESCO, 1993.
10. G. Pourcet, *Les problèmes du développement à Madagascar* [Development Problems in Madagascar], Paris, Université de Paris X, 1991–92. (DESS course paper.)

The major changes which are taking place in this area form part of the overall body of strategies and measures to be defined and implemented for integrated development, perhaps in a medium- or long-term perspective, but with cultural factors and effects that will have to be taken fully into consideration.

Analyses of this kind are easier to make at the local level or even in a specific sector. Allowance for cultural factors obviously becomes increasingly complex as we move on to national development policies – where the integration and interaction of the proposed measures assume central importance – or to international co-operation strategies and projects.

The very scale of the operations and geographical territory involved necessitates, on the one hand, decentralization to ensure that decisions are effectively implemented and, on the other, identification of the shared cultural features of a particular geographical area, so as to enable general recommendations to be included in the proposed plans or programmes for development.

This whole complex of problems requires new approaches and procedures which will enable cultural factors to be integrated into development strategies, plans, policies and projects. These will be the subject of Part Three of this review.

The integration of cultural factors into development: means, methods and instruments

Introduction

As we saw in Part One of this study, significant progress was made in the 1980s, even though that progress remains limited. The methods of analysis (checklists) are either incomplete, too general or too complicated for easy practical use. Moreover, the consideration of qualitative aspects presents difficult problems for the preparation of programmes and projects arrived at by conventional planning methods. In addition, the importance of the human and cultural objectives of development seems far from the thoughts of the major economic or political players.

This was why, in Part Two of this study, we made a detailed analysis of the cultural factors and effects of development and, in particular, looked at the interactions at work in this area, with the object of systematizing the comment and observations already made regarding the component elements of different cultures.

Part Three presents a series of appropriate resources, methods and instruments in response to the concern of decision-makers wanting to make a special effort to give cultural aspects their rightful place among the various factors of development. With that end in view, decision-makers must be enabled to grasp the practical side of these aspects and the diversity of the human groups which they reflect. It will then be possible for them to translate these aspects into programmable elements so that they can be integrated into projects designed to improve the living standards and conditions of the populations concerned.

What is more, development decision-makers have to be able to assess the overall impact of development actions at the outcome of the programme and in the longer-term perspective typical of the evolution of societies. Here we attempt to put forward a few pre-liminary answers to this need under two headings: first, we propose a number of working instruments and, in some cases, open the debate on the use of methods and instruments designed to permit concrete identification of the cultural aspects which interact with development; second, we discuss the evaluation of the short- and long-term impact of development on every aspect of the life of a human group expressed through its culture; and, last, it is proposed that account be taken of the cultural similarities and differences in programmes directed at broad geocultural areas.

Thus, the close relations that exist between the economy and culture lead to recognition of the fact that no development project can afford to disregard the cultural dimension. Although positive and negative interactions are intuitively evident between culture and development, they are highly complex and difficult to grasp and analyse. Only a global, multidisciplinary study and an all-round approach can reveal the contradictions and complementarities which typify the multifaceted relations between culture and development.

It has to be repeated that there is certainly no 'one' methodology for taking the cultural dimension of development into account. There is certainly no quantitative method for doing so completely. For the purposes of development decision-makers, however, there are a number of approaches, instruments and methods – some of which are already used in part, but separately from the study of the interactions between culture and development – which can be proposed to them so that these interactions can be taken into account in the different types of forward planning documents – for example, strategies, programmes, policies and projects. With that end in view we shall now deal in turn with:

- the main features of a cultural approach possible in any kind of document;
- adjustments to current methods of forecasting, implementation and evaluation, i.e. planning, regardless of the type of document concerned;
- specific instruments (indicators and evaluation techniques for fieldwork);
- last but not least, general instruments which are also useful at every level of planning. They enable concrete evidence to be given of cultural factors, while also representing the institutional side (decision-making process) of the project cycle, the relative

weight of each participant in the overall process ('globalization', systems analysis, etc.), the cultural context for implementation (cultural areas) and, finally, the long-term impact (scenario method, long-range forecasting).

Apart from the strictly methodological propositions, a number of conditions and guidelines will be outlined for:

- an interdisciplinary approach based on experience of project observation and evaluation;
- training decision-makers and other actors in development to make them more aware of the cultural implications of their tasks;
- last but not least, the fostering of participation by the population in development. This is a subject to which reference is often made, but it tends to elicit a set of questions instead of proposing 'ready-to-use' solutions to the difficulties of the dialogue between 'developers' and 'developed'.

CHAPTER 8

A cultural approach to development planning policies and processes

In general the main forecasting and planning documents drawn up by development agencies give only limited consideration to the cultural dimension, which is not properly integrated into the analyses or action plans – for which a rigorous presentation is generally adopted. Worse still, cultural factors never constitute the foundation or the goals of the proposals which are formulated, as though the realities to which they refer were ultimately insignificant or unfathomable.

Regardless of the type of document envisaged (strategies, programmes or projects) it is therefore essential to adopt a cultural approach to the problems of the economic and social development of a human group or society. This implies, first of all, that these problems cannot, even for human or humanitarian purposes, be identified externally or conceptualized on the basis of analyses and methods deployed in a totally different intellectual and institutional context that proposes to deal with problems which have no relation to the real-life existence of the populations concerned. A development project or programme can only be identified in conjunction with the population itself and on the basis of its patterns of life, thought and action. Similarly any action designed to improve the conditions and standard of living of the population must be based on its practices, aptitudes and knowledge in the economic and social – as well as other – spheres.

In brief, a radically new perspective must be adopted: the existing cultural experience of a population must be the point of departure for the design and implementation of development; preconceived notions and models cannot be used, even in the area of human development, with the addition, by way of an afterthought, of partial cultural references which are bound to remain superficial and lack any organic link with the proposed strategies and actions.

Background documents

STRATEGIC DOCUMENTS: THE UNITED NATIONS INTERNATIONAL DEVELOPMENT STRATEGY

Allowance for non-economic factors and the use of cultural references did evolve in the 1970s and 1980s. However, the basic structure of the Strategy for the 1990s, the aims and goals assigned to the United Nations system and the policies and measures advocated still fall far short of a cultural approach or, in other words, the requirements of truly integrated development.

The Preamble identifies development problems as follows: a widening gulf between the rich and poor countries, youth unemployment, the spread of violence, drug abuse and illness, and increasingly serious damage to the environment. These problems all have a bearing on the search for sustainable development. However, no explicit mention is made of the cultural goals of development or of the need to consider the cultural factors in the quest for solutions to these problems, in spite of the fact that all have a major cultural dimension.

In the fight against poverty, for example, it is wrong to consider the poor as having no culture, knowledge or expertise. The Strategy should include recommendations which take account of these factors in order to prevent development aid from being designed, put into effect and perceived as purely external assistance. If it is to attain its goal, the aid system should on the contrary be based on the participation and mobilization of the local human potential and on specific local techniques and ways of doing things. Similarly, measures in favour of human rights must always allow for the cultural and social models that exist in different societies, which themselves are constantly changing.

Turning now to the fundamental objectives set for the United Nations Decade for Development for the 1990s, explicit reference is admittedly made to participation, protection of cultural diversity and human rights, yet the approaches and aims defined for the

156

attainment of these broad objectives remain essentially economic.

And the economy is precisely the sector in which cultural factors – such as the models, value systems and traditions which govern local economic activities – must be identified, recognized and seen, in some cases, as factors of potential development which are just as significant as a modern economy. As to ecological problems, their perception varies widely from one society and culture to another. A range of educational methods and policies should therefore be developed as a function of the cultural context specific to each type of society and, more specifically, the patterns of behaviour, modes of consumption and environmental management system rooted in its culture.

The priorities which are laid down in the policies and measures recommended by the Strategy relate essentially to the stimulation of development through economic and financial resources. Thus, no mention is made of the cultural dimension or, more importantly, the cultural impact of the problems, objectives, policies and measures which are announced, although the significance of this dimension should be almost self-evident in some cases – particularly in the areas of education, family planning policy and health – its translation into economic and financial terms coming only second in order.

The long-term objectives assigned to the United Nations Decade might therefore include: the development of societies and cultures in their own right, respect for cultural diversity, dialogue and intercultural co-operation. Culture might also constitute the 'transverse' dimension of the whole set of policies and measures proposed to relaunch the development process. Finally, the half-way assessment of the results of the Strategy should in future include a study of its sociocultural impact.

However, it is at the level of the very foundations of the Strategy that the need arises for a far-reaching reappraisal of the existing concepts and procedures, setting out from the notion of the interaction between culture and development. First of all, the cultural dimension of the international situation might be assessed in terms of the challenges – demographic, economic, social and cultural – as recalled in the introduction to this review. The *World Report on Culture and Development* being prepared by the World Commission on Culture and Development will, without doubt, make an important contribution here. The cultural causes and effects of the challenges in the area of demography and the economy might be brought to light and genuinely integrated into the overall study. The Strategy might go on to describe the probable major trends of cultural, economic and social evolution over the next ten years. Finally, it might recommend the types of action to be taken in these different areas to attenuate the negative effects of the expected changes in the context of integrated development. These actions could of course only be described in very broad outline, in the form of guidelines or recommendations. These would be addressed in particular to the member agencies of the United Nations system, which would use them to establish their own programmes.

In this way the organizations and bodies concerned would be acting on the Resolution adopted by the United Nations General Assembly, proclaiming the World Decade for Cultural Development, which called upon them to work more particularly towards the attainment of its first objective, that is, acknowledging the cultural dimension of development.

PROGRAMME DOCUMENTS OF INSTITUTIONS ENGAGED
IN INTERNATIONAL DEVELOPMENT CO-OPERATION

The issues referred to above in relation to the United Nations Strategy also concern the Specialized Agencies of the United Nations system. In their case clear reference to the cultural dimension of development could be made in medium-term planning or general documents concerning the five-year programme cycles and even in the annual *UNDP Human Development Report*, the central concept of which would acquire its full value if it gave material space to cultural aspects and factors. As to the programme documents themselves, the cultural dimension could well be fitted into terms of reference and the description of implementation policies and measures in the form of main policy thrusts (regularities) and general recommendations, whose content would however apply to all projects stemming from the programmes.

To the extent that documents of this type contain little if any statistical data, cultural factors could be included more readily, since they would be one of the major, or even structural, elements of the 'terms of reference' and, at a later stage, of the strategies and major policy guidelines for the attainment of goals that are still relatively global.

In the explanatory memoranda, the cultural dimension would therefore first be included in the outline of the general problem area that is the justification for the proposed strategies and policies. At this stage it would be presented in both descriptive and normative terms (see above).

The inclusion of cultural factors – both as cause and effect in the development process – might also be one of the long-term or major objectives of this type of document. Here reference could be made to the principal objectives of the World Decade for Cultural Development, each of which is a facet of the Decade's first and principal objective (affirmation and enrichment of cultural identities, broader participation in cultural life in the broad sense and promotion of international cultural co-operation as means and end of the World Decade for Cultural Development through a more intensive dialogue and intercultural solidarity).

The cultural dimension would then be taken up again in its dual role as an accelerator, as well as a potential source of tensions and conflicts, in the formulation of the strategies which 'surround' and guide policies and programme measures for development in the various areas of economic and social life.

Finally, in the description of specific or sectoral policies and measures, a 'transverse' theme – that is, one that is common to all the different sectoral actions – would take up the main headings of the definition of culture laid down at MONDIACULT: traditions and beliefs, value systems, fundamental human rights, ways of life, arts and letters (or rather, forms and role of cultural and artistic expression). In that connection, the craft trades and cultural industries might figure among the economic activities which are capable of creating employment and earning currency. At all events, attention would be drawn to the concrete interaction between these elements and development activities.

Planned programmes of activities for shorter periods (one or two years) might include activities based explicitly and concretely on the interaction between culture and development, as described in Part Two under the heading 'Priority Areas of Application and New Strategies' (savings, business enterprise, the informal economy, agriculture, basic education, health action, housing, promotion of the role of women, the environment and population).

Development projects

For the most part, the directives given by development agencies such as UNDP only include headings covering the conventional phases of project definition in terms of justification, goals, anticipated outcomes, activities, resources, duration and evaluation. The only heading under which cultural aspects might be included is entitled 'Situation of the Country', but it seems unlikely that information of this type will be entered here unless precise instructions are given to that end.

Here mention should be made of the directives produced by UNESCO for the drafting of project documents concerning funds-in-trust. Also relevant to some extent are the UNDP directives on processes for participation in the drafting of project documents. The general heading 'Special Considerations' asks for the inclusion of special observations concerning project impact on the promotion of equality between men and women, the environment and the cultural dimension of development. This latter subject might be dealt with by taking over the main components of the definition of culture given in Part Two here: traditions and beliefs, value systems, norms of social and economic organization, ways of life and artistic expression.[1]

The way in which the various project participants are to be mobilized is also closely bound up with the cultural dimension of the future project. The preparation of a bilateral or multilateral co-operation project in fact brings together, at the conceptual and decision-making stages: national technical and political decision-makers, external fund providers, domestic and foreign consultants and experts, and NGOs, as the case may be. However, the target population is rarely, if ever, a party to the discussions.

In the identification of the project, feasibility studies and negotiation, these participants all use arguments and methods and define objectives related to their professional, financial, economic and political roles and based on a solidly rational approach.

---

1. UNDP, *Guidelines for Development Projects,* UNDP, 1992; UNESCO, *Operational Project Evaluation,* Paris, UNESCO, 1992. (UNESCO doc. CEU/Inf. Series/9-Rev.)

However, the project obviously also implies other 'downstream' participants: local authority employees; local businesses, associations and organizations; and the beneficiaries, who ought to be identified in advance: their needs and their norms (values, behaviour patterns, social organization, etc.) need to be taken into account from the earliest possible moment in the preparation of the project.

Already in the design stage it is not always possible to achieve a consensus among the parties involved at the local level or between the national and local, and institutional and community levels. When the first document or 'paper project' is drafted (goals, constraints, resources, financing, planning and legal, institutional and technical basis), the financial decision-makers, politicians, technicians and NGO officials apply different and sometimes even divergent points of view, which have to be converted into a final compromise.

But when the implementation stage is reached, the 'field project' comes up against the population and the reactions of the grass-roots participants. Based on the evaluation of a large number of projects, what happens at this stage falls, most frequently, under one of the following headings:

- unconditional acceptance of certain innovations as forecast – generally low-risk and therefore quickly adopted by the people;
- selective adoption within a broader set of proposals, often due to the fact that the spread of a new practice very largely depends on the prior adoption of another innovation;
- adoption with provisos;
- adoption with amendments to initial objectives;
- rejection of the proposed innovations when highly speculative and therefore high-risk.

In fact, acceptance or rejection is often explained by the possibilities which exist for risk management, the interests at stake and the expected gain, and also by the fact that some innovations require a change in the organization of work with a degree of social upheaval. Even so, some innovations which are rapidly accepted may also lead to extensive social change. This shows that the populations concerned – and in the first instance peasant communities – are, subject to certain conditions, willing to accept innovations proposed by outside agencies. The cultural factor naturally plays a role here. The populations embody these innovations in their system of expectations and mental images and their material and social situation.

If genuine allowance is made for cultural factors in development programmes and projects, the planning methods as such must first be reappraised. Their present logic does not permit this integration because of the rigidity of the time horizons for a particular project, the types of decision it involves, the goals set and the nature of the results or effects that are evaluated.

It follows that, regardless of the type of document concerned, the reappraisal must cover all the planning techniques, ranging in order over all the successive phases of a development programme, plan or project: identification, preparation (including *ex ante* assessment), decision-making, implementation and *ex post* assessment. The problems encountered concern activities corresponding to these different phases of work.

PREPARATORY PHASE

Identification and preparation

Identification of the criteria for the programming and preparation of projects itself poses a series of questions to the extent that this is the key to all planning.

The first precondition for the viability of a development project is correct identification of its components and objectives. Observation of the behaviour patterns of the participants in local life, the problems they encounter and the solutions conceived and applied by them constitute the basic information which can be given formal shape in a project after collation and setting in order. A development project therefore cannot be founded on theoretical suppositions or purely external hypotheses. Similarly, the cultural and sociocultural characteristics which are to be mobilized in the project can only be identified *in situ*. The detail in which these conditions can be respected will, of course, not be the same with a wide-scale project as it can be for a micro-project.

Evaluation or preliminary study

For the preliminary (*ex ante*) study, from which the general problem area and action priorities for the plan will be defined, a number of questions have to be answered. What is to be the role of documentation and what kind of data will be required? What part is to be played by the *ex post* assessments at the different hierarchical levels? What type of information are they to contain? Are there any other mechanisms for information feedback: expert reports or studies by scientific specialists? How are they used and summarized for the *ex ante* evaluation? On what forward data is this evaluation based?

It would be highly desirable for the *ex ante* evaluations to include, first, a detailed description of any previous activities related to those programmed, even in areas outside their specific field of application, and, second, information on the cultural situation of the country in which the project is to be set in place and on major medium-term international cultural and economic trends.

This is all the more important as, following the classic model, programming must be planned in advance. In every case action follows programming and must, in principle, conform to it. The objectives set are to be attained within time limits defined in compliance with the norms laid down, all uncertainty being reduced to the minimum.

However, this planning, reassuring as it is for the 'developer', is not true to the real situation in the field or to the reactions of the target groups to be 'developed'. They are confronted with many daily needs which cannot be foreseen in detail, and with precarious conditions of material insecurity; they are motivated by their own cultural experience and form part of a specific power relationship. The target groups will therefore react to events as they occur, in an apparently erratic manner and by a process of successive adjustment as opportunities arise. In a sense they practise a kind of reverse planning, *ex post*, by the very way in which they use or participate in the project. It is therefore essential to allow some flexibility and even a possible change of aim at the time the project document is being finalized.

Determination of the goals and priorities should be based on the results of the *ex ante* evaluation of the project's foreseeable product and effects. The priorities for the coming programming period will also be decided on the same basis. Using an integrative approach, that is, taking the non-economic factors of development and their interactions into account, various methods already widely used for rationalization of budget choices and in business strategies can be used for analysing problems – by which is meant breaking them down into their constituent parts and their interactions with other problems. A study of the various possible combinations then leads on to a study of the relationship between ends and means in strategic terms and to the formulation of a structure of programme goals.

Many different planning methods have been designed and applied for economic purposes, but their very nature and the predominance of the quantitative formulation of objectives and results make it impossible to adapt them to a cultural approach to development problems. It is worth presenting one of them, however, known as intervention planning by objectives (IPO), as an instrument for determining what action to take, because the method requires that the actions be determined in conjunction with the population concerned.

The IPO method, first designed by USAID (and called Logical Framework Analysis) and developed by the technical co-operation agency (GTZ) of the German Ministry for Economic Co-operation (BMZ) is more and more widely used (World Bank, UNDP, EU, national ministries, NGOs, etc.). True, it does not provide a wholly satisfactory answer to the problem of taking the cultural dimension of development into account, but it does propose a useful methodology for participative planning because it involves representatives of target groups in the framework of the analysis phase which brings together, on the same level, all the players concerned by the question being studied. Problems are then converted collectively, using critical path analysis, into a 'problem tree', which – in its turn – is translated into an 'objectives tree' from which the action logic is deduced.

At all events, it is a way of setting operational objectives and determining the expected results or products in a project document. It takes into account effective needs as perceived by the population, thus enabling its own cultural values to be given consideration and at the same time the opportunities for it to be involved in the implementation of the project. This could make the drafting of the relevant parts of the project that much easier.

This method does, however, have its limitations owing to the inequalities between those carrying out the project and its beneficiaries. It is the former, in collaboration with the national authorities and the providers of the finance, who decide on the sets of problems to be dealt with and the financial incidence of the operation. The implicit criteria for the 'developers''choices therefore still predominate. Lastly, the implementation of the projects is not necessarily in the hands of the populations concerned or their representatives. The advantages of the method, therefore, are a matter of the flexibility of the planning processes and the complex problem of the population's effective participation in its own development.[2]

IMPLEMENTATION

Three major questions arise in the phase of plan or programme implementation proper.

Decentralization

The degree of decentralization (of initiative, services and resources) counterbalances what is still the centralized nature of decision-making as far as the major institutions are concerned because of their very size, the geographical scale of their activities and the relative importance of the sums of money involved. To that extent, decentralization has the advantage of closeness to the 'ground', thus making it easier to see development problems in the concrete terms of the societies where they arise. However, the problems this creates should not be underestimated: relations with the governments concerned, pressure groups, a weakening in the coherence of the project and the difficulty in building up co-ordination between the various levels of decision and the 'ground'.

In spite of these risks, the fact remains that a development programme or plan cannot throw deep roots into the local environment unless it enjoys the active co-operation (or the benevolent neutrality) of the local authorities and uses the existing sociocultural structures, both traditional (the ancients) and modern (voluntary co-operative movements). But it is important not to 'graft' co-operative structures on to community structures where there is no compatibility between the two. In this connection, the question of action by the NGOs, whose lightweight structures and close contact with the people may constitute an irreplaceable link, has to be treated separately. Here, a distinction has to be drawn between the big NGOs, whose size and resources may weigh heavily on the operational value of the actions undertaken, and the small field NGOs, more closely tailored to actual needs precisely because of their smallness.

2.   See E. Sizoo, *Quid pro quo* (Brussels), No. 10/11, September 1992.

Duration of the project

The time-scale of the project also plays a major role in its chances of success. Given the differences in different population groups' perception of time, knowledge of the facts suggests that variable planning durations or 'sliding' plans should be proposed, together with ways of renewing programmes on terms and with objectives that may be the same or revised but, at all events, are adjusted to the real time taken by complex operations involving deep-reaching changes. Actually this flexibility is already apparent in certain of UNDP's procedures, in the form of the revision and rephasing of some of its projects, when it is clear that the practical conditions for their implementation, possibly of a sociocultural nature, may affect the results and have not been sufficiently allowed for at the outset.

Indeed, one of the main difficulties that development projects come up against is the absence of unity in the time-scale and pace of the action by the different partners. Awareness campaigns, training activities and the rate at which each project becomes implanted are directly dependent on the cultural dimension. On the one hand, the 'time' of the planner has a horizon sometimes of one year and generally limited to five. What is more, the time available for meetings, decisions, contracts, information campaigns and targeted operations is necessarily short, whilst, on the other hand, the transformation of attitudes, acceptance of technical change and reorganization of collective activities take place at an even but always slow pace. A project must therefore integrate these different perceptions of time, which are incompatible with linear updating.

Flexibility

Flexibility must also be the general rule in the implementation of a programme. The programme must be flexible right from the forecasting stage and open to change and adaptation as a function of the objective factors which facilitate or obstruct its implementation. It must be possible to envisage fall-back solutions as regards both the procedures and the goals of the programmed action. An adequate budgetary reserve therefore needs to be set aside to cope with these changes. In other words, the system of 'tied aid', that is, the allocation of funding to actions described in detail, should be used only in part, with the remaining credits being assigned in no less binding a way but according to more general allocation criteria.

It is at this stage that periodical evaluations may prove useful, while the programme is in progress. Similarly, the different paths that could be followed in implementing the project need to have been envisaged at the forecasting stage. In this regard, simulation techniques and alternative scenarios may be useful.

Ex post *or final evaluation*

The *ex post* evaluation of a development programme or plan is one of the most important phases of its implementation, provided that a number of conditions are respected: the evaluation must not simply be a report on the actions taken, but also – and perhaps primarily – take the form of the evaluation of the effects of these actions in the particular area involved and on economic, social and cultural sectors in their entirety. The assessment must therefore be at three levels:

- evaluation of the *outcomes* in terms of efficiency and 'effectiveness' (anticipated/achieved outcomes);
- evaluation of expected and unexpected *effects* in the sphere of action itself or over a much larger area (sociocultural effects of a development project, for example), including unfavourable secondary effects (e.g. giving up food crops for cash crops resulting in dependence on external sources);
- evaluation of the in-depth *impact* (in the sense of shock) and lasting long-term effects (sometimes unpredictable).

In addition, in-depth surveys may be carried out (participation research, and also studies summarizing changes in lifestyles and cultural, ethical and spiritual value systems). Clearly such assessments can only be arrived at in the medium or even long term. In the field, however, changes may be more easily detectable.

Ideally, it would be desirable for the evaluation process to accompany the project throughout all its phases:

- *ex ante* evaluation (initial study), as we have already seen, designed to identify problems, set objectives, ways and means, and forecast the direct and indirect results and effects of the programme;
- concomitant evaluation (monitoring progress) to check the practical value of the reasoning adopted and the resources made available, correcting and adjusting, where necessary, the

procedures and content of the action taken and re-aligning the objectives set at the start;

- lastly, the final or *ex post* evaluation (see above), designed to draw lessons from the implementation of the programme and to take them into account in the construction of future programmes (renew, amend or stop). As we have seen, the *ex post* evaluation may be one of the references used in drafting the *ex ante* evaluation for the next phase of action.

CHAPTER 9

Aids to decision-making

Over and above the techniques of planning as such, the drafting of
forecasting documents in the field of development requires – if its
cultural factors and effects are to be clearly grasped – that decision-
makers' choices be clarified on a number of points. These points are
essential if the choices made are to take effective account of cultural
factors among all the others (mainly economic and political) that
help towards the project's success. For more general reasons, of a
human or even ethical nature, decision-makers need to be informed
about the induced effects (moral, social and cultural) of their action.
  They therefore need to have tools enabling them to:
* identify the concrete features of a population's culture (or that
  of a given geocultural area);
* have an overall assessment of all the actors and factors involved
  in the development process;
* analyse the foreseeable long-term effects of development on the
  culture of a given society.
There are a number of methods and instruments available for the
purpose, designed to deal not necessarily with this specific problem
but with some features possibly applicable to the integration of cultural factors in development. The instruments concerned, the interest of which resides largely in the 'macro' approach to problems,
relate to the following fields: analysis of decision-making processes;
'operationalization' of cultural factors; 'globalization' of development problems; creation or strengthening of continuous flows of
information on the 'situation in the field'; and the geographical distribution of cultural features.
  However, some of these instruments apply more particularly to

169

project documentation. These are the cultural indicators (or perception/tension factors) of development, assessment techniques (cost/benefit and cost/effectiveness analysis, etc.) and, finally, tables and models for testing the cultural acceptability of development projects with a given population.

Analysis of decision-making processes

It is clear from observation that development assistance institutions and the big economic and political decision-makers, particularly at the international level, fail to grasp the importance of the non-economic or social factors and effects of development or to re-aim their analyses and strategies beyond improving the living conditions of a population through economic growth, education and a higher standard of living. The same applies to public and private sector decision-makers at the national or local level. All in all, they fail to take on board everything specifically related to culture.

Conversely, fieldworkers (in particular, co-operation personnel from the industrialized countries) often complain of incomprehension at two levels:

• that of the local population, whose experience and ways of thinking cannot be brought 'into phase' with the pragmatic approach necessary for the implementation of a development project without a long period of training and considerable ability to communicate;

• that of the funding sources (even the offices of the co-operation agencies to whom they are responsible), the difficulty being to feed them back information and to get them to take it into account.

According to the fieldworkers, ensuring that this type of information was taken into account would necessarily mean generating another type of project, which would aim beyond the purely technical aspects and involve a better reflection of the realities and complexity of local situations.

The situation, therefore, is one of broken communications stemming from two facts: firstly, the way in which development decisions are made and passed on to fieldworkers, and secondly, without doubt, the quantitative and qualitative shortfall in the requests, evaluations and data fed back from the field to high-level decision-makers to inform them of the factual situation – particularly in the economic, social and cultural environment they are working in – the effects of their action and the 'needs' or problems not yet met or resolved.

Here the question of the general approach to problems arises: should it be from the top down or from the bottom up? In other words, the choice is between centralized systems and the definition of projects and programmes in the field, that is, identification of problems at source.[1]

As regards decision-making on master development programmes at the top, the choices made cannot be conceived with the cultural approach necessary to bring about effective changes in the situation on the ground unless they are based on the views of an expert group or research team qualified in social and human sciences and able to deal with the cultural aspects of development problems.

Given the relatively short time available to development organizations to make their decisions, it will also be essential to have adequate and relevant information which must be as up to date and as condensed and to the point as possible, reflecting the different facets of reality and their impact on the non-economic aspects of the development programmes under consideration. In that connection, a whole range of instruments needs to be made available to decision-makers, directly or via their research departments: sets of cultural indicators of development, experiments in 'operationalizing' cultural factors, alternative scenarios, 'global' analyses of development, and studies in long-range development forecasting enabling the interplay between actors and factors to be 're-composed'. It would also, perhaps, be useful to envisage the plotting of a map of cultural areas, which help take into account the significant similarities or dissimilarities of cultures in territories for which development programmes are planned, at different geographical levels. The setting up of specialized data banks and observatories could also be considered. On another level, the existence of informal intelligence networks could also be very useful for high-level decision-making. Here resource persons with valuable knowledge and experience in the field can be an irreplaceable source of information.

1. See D. Desjeux, *Dimension culturelle et aide à la décision* [The Cultural Dimension and Aid to Decision-making], Part 1, Paris, UNESCO, 1993.

However, although this sophistication of instruments at the top of the tree is useful, the problem of the institutional, geographical and cultural gap between decision and action and the scale of observation of world realities – i.e. economic or sociocultural observation at the level of the great international strategies or in the field – will have a considerable impact on the anticipated outcomes.

The greater this gap and the more numerous the intervening echelons, the greater the likelihood of decisions being deformed, bearings lost and the power of the initial thrust weakened along the way. Above all, however, the more general the scale of observation the greater the risk of overlooking differences, underrating difficulties and, more particularly, failing to perceive the strengths and weaknesses of a specific society or culture. As a result, the cultural criteria chosen at the highest level of responsibility will be too general to allow for the specific features of a situation in the field, which is bound to be diversified. This brings to mind the evaluation carried out by UNICEF in 1986 on its programme for African children, which brought out the lack of coherence and the major contradictions between projects as planned and implemented by the national authorities or bi- and multilateral co-operation agencies in this field and the actual potential and drawbacks in local cultural and material contexts (see p. 55).

Here we are once again faced with the problems of the decentralization of decision-making and action and those of the fundamental difference between the fieldworker who sees the concrete work of people for their development by and via their culture and the decision-maker who cannot, of necessity, be exposed to all this rich experience. This is why all channels of information on this subject need to be catalogued and used and why the effort must be made to draw up summaries on the features of and recent problems with development issues in the area concerned, where applicable on the basis of case-studies and evaluation reports.

Lastly, as we shall see later, with participation, negotiation and dialogue with the population all under way, it will be possible at the very least to provide the 'developers' with tangible information on the way the people with whom they have to work think and live. It must not be forgotten, however, that it is rare for field information to be passed on from national level to the intermediate or highest levels of the international organizations.

Understanding the culture of a population as a tangible reality

While all the elements which go to make up a particular culture are virtually present in any analysis of the systems of values, beliefs and ways of life and thought which characterize that culture, they are, in part at least and especially in everyday life, implicit or else unspoken – being in the realm of what people do not talk about. While some cultures are more extrovert than others, it is only in certain circumstances that cultural traits normally not visible and serving, in practice, to mark the difference between two cultures are exhibited, mentioned or even flaunted.

This does not mean that such traits are not felt to be important: quite the contrary. But it is only when this reference to culture is necessary that it is made. This is the case in situations of conflict in general and in development 'situations' in particular. Here there is no need for the individual or social dimension of culture to be taken into account in all its complexity. All that is needed is a brief summary to uncover certain 'regular' features, neither too general nor too detailed, such as the relationship of the people to their own bodies, religion, health and food (see next chapter).

But these are still macro-social tools. To reach field level, we need to start from the real practices of the people concerned or the local decision-makers, their value scales and hierarchy and therefore their preferences as participants as a function of their lifestyles, education, traditions and beliefs. The results of these 'utility surveys' come, in their turn, into the social interplay of negotiation, for example between 'developers' and 'developed', so that the decision to retain, strengthen, change or halt a given development programme is based on the open knowledge of truly cultural or socio-cultural factors.

Here a fundamental distinction has to be drawn between need and desirability or interest. The meaning of 'need' – in all populations and regardless of economic, social and political context – is vague and ambiguous. Actually, it is always difficult to say what one does not have – and still more what one does not know. What is more, 'developers' have been known to substitute their own list of legitimate requirements for what the population perceive as being needed. Conversely, individuals are always found to react positively to an external proposal if they see it as being in their interest. The

173

existence of a need is not enough. The real interest (desirability) of a population in a project can be discovered by analysing the sacrifices, contributions and return that beneficiaries are prepared to make for its implementation by spontaneously mobilizing their resources. The interests present reveal the different forces at work in the group and one need may overlap divergent interests through the challenge it offers to the social structures and power relations.[2] Thus, for instance, from 1975 to 1993, the Environment Development Association (ENDA-GRAF) ran a development programme centred on the people in a popular quarter of Dakar – Grand-Yoff – with a population of over 100,000. One of the actions in this programme was to sink 1,000 sumps to collect waste water. The operation was to be carried out in conjunction with the health committee of the quarter, the object being to improve drainage.

However, the programme met with two opposite types of attitude on the part of the population. Residents needed the sumps but only the landlords were interested in their being built, tenants being reluctant or even against, knowing they could not be moved out and that the availability or otherwise of the sumps would do nothing to improve their economic or social position. This simple fact clearly explains the reason for the opposing attitudes and shows how interest carries more weight than need and is stronger operationally.[3]

This explains why populations sometimes follow strategies designed to frustrate and divert, to divide and to cloud public opinion in order to protect themselves from external intervention, safeguard their own security and absorb external help to suit specific internal mechanisms and rationalities. This also explains the misunderstandings and quarrels between fieldworkers and populations.[4]

Similarly, the notion of strategy implies that human attitudes are governed by self-interest, whether material or symbolic, and that, in order to bring about and negotiate a change, the interests at play and what is at stake – i.e. what everyone stands to win or lose – therefore have to have been understood. Strategy also implies that

2. See Desjeux, op. cit.
3. See H. Panhuys, E. Sizoo and T. Verhelst, *La prise en compte des facteurs culturels dans les projets de développement* [Taking Cultural Factors into Account in Development Programmes], pp. 11-16, Paris, UNESCO, 1993. (UNESCO doc. CLT-93/WS/3.)
4. Desjeux, op. cit.

the players are caught up in a social game which is both undefined and structured by the other players involved. In the general approach it includes the interests of officials, developers and decision-makers and the rationality of the population. But this approach does not make it easy to cover anything of an affective or irrational nature or, like the systems approach, anything under the heading of disorder or breakdown.[5]

In general terms cultural factors are taken into account in reaching development choices (in this instance at local level only) in three different ways:

- clarifying cultural values by reducing them to questions of utility or self-interest as a function of the population's response and reactions to specific issues;
- bringing out the social or cultural utility of the proposed options (no longer simply by cost-benefit analysis);
- applying a procedure for negotiation between development officials and local populations, bearing in mind the limits of all participation experiments bound up with other elements of the culture of the populations concerned, the scale of the proposed changes, the authority of the decision-makers and the economic and social interest of the change.

It is not easy to transpose this method to a higher level, given the hierarchical differences between the players involved and the difficulty of arriving at a synthesis of the different scales of preference. At this level it is sometimes possible to be satisfied with only general information about the main cultural or sociocultural features of the area where action is proposed. Resource persons could also be consulted in order to throw light on certain aspects of the situation that are not too clear to the experts on their own. Lastly, the method of 'globalizing' development might be used.

5.   D. Desjeux, *Essay on Training in Culture*, Paris, UNESCO, 1990. (UNESCO doc. CC/CSP/CP/22.)

Understanding the overall interaction between culture and development

Necessary as it is, at the level of operations in the field, to individualize the cultural factors of development and bring them out in practical terms, so is it just as essential, at the macro level, for decision-makers to be in a position to paint for themselves a complete picture of their role and of the action they are carrying out among all the other players and actions contributing to the development programme. This is the only way in which they will be able to weigh up the real relevance and impact of their decisions by locating them in the complexity characteristic of any development situation. This exercise, part of the tools of planning at macro level, means having to resort to theorization but, on the other hand, presents the advantage of providing the high-level decision-makers with an overall picture of the context in which their choices are set.

This self-assessment therefore entails a repositioning of all the participants and actions involved in development, understood as a dynamic process extending over a certain length of time.

This proposition meets the need for the high-level decision-maker to think out what he will do, not in terms of specialization and in a sectoral manner, but as part of a whole and, where the field and people are concerned, as an action that will have multiple direct and indirect effects in what is by definition a complex reality.

The exercise may be seen as an attempt at modelization, provided the fact is accepted that it is not a question of representing the reality of the decision and its environment but, on the contrary, of limiting it to what seems relevant to understanding what most influences a decision. However, the need to conceive of development as a multidimensional process makes it necessary to attempt to define and show the relationship between several different types of behavioural logic and several levels of reality – biological, sociological and anthropological. The method enables one to grasp all the factors that contribute to a development process aimed at innovating without destroying.[6]

6. B. Clergerie, *Synoptic Report on the Regional Seminar on the Cultural Dimension of Development in Africa*, Paris, UNESCO, 1992.

It can also prove useful to employ systems analysis, if not the 'systems' or even the 'culture' approach,[7] so as to provide decision-makers with an overall view of the actions to be carried out and their possible effects.

SYSTEMS ANALYSIS

Systems analysis, in a dynamic perspective, is founded on the idea of feedback, which assumes that a person reacts and then adapts. Its advantage is that it implies a linkage between the elements of the system: changing one element of the system starts a chain reaction causing changes on a greater or lesser scale in part or in the whole of the rest of the system. However, it is difficult for systems analysis to include discontinuity and, in particular, any link between the rational and the irrational and between reason and emotion. Even so, it does help to demonstrate that a technical decision – to adopt an innovation in agriculture, for example – is not only technical but also has cultural implications. It shows that a technique or a plant are elements in a vaster whole, that is, the production system, which is itself an integral part of the social system.

THE 'NETWORKS' APPROACH

The network notion makes it possible to work on communications, the dissemination of information and negotiation between players on the principle that, however individual a decision may appear to be, it is, above all else, an effect of a social network. The mental images that the players form of themselves and each other emerge from interactive information circulating in the networks. The approach also allows the informal sector, that is the often scarcely apparent 'informal' networks that structure an organization or village beyond the formal hierarchies, to be studied. It often helps in understanding the procedures whereby the cultural models for solving problems can be constructed, beyond bureaucratic appearances, and how, finally, people are able to adapt. The approach can also be useful in assisting farmers to think about what they do. However, it often has a tendency to underestimate power relations among participants.

7. See Desjeux, *Essay on training . . .*, op. cit.

177

THE 'CULTURE' APPROACH

This approach starts from two observations, firstly in terms of inter-action (how different rationalities interacting, for example between technicians and peasants, are self-regulating or not), and secondly in terms of meaning (how individuals project themselves and iden-tify with their own culture through values, symbols, social rituals, language, etc.). This approach today is fairly routinely applied to peasant thinking, particularly by anthropologists, but far less at the level of organizations and therefore technicians and the decision-makers themselves.

These various approaches, together with the 'strategy' ap-proach, enable development workers to 'manage' cultural differen-ces better so that they can see human reality in a different light, for example, the role of the subconscious, the informal, the social links between participants and differences in thinking patterns.

A long-term approach to the evolution of cultures and societies

The problems of society and cultural change in their interaction with development processes cannot be assessed accurately in a short- or medium-term perspective. The very notion of sustainable development requires a long-term view of development problems and policies. Though certain very rapid economic and technical changes have immediate social and cultural consequences, the fun-damental features of cultures and societies change very slowly and cannot be identified except in the long term. And yet this is gener-ally the pace at which the most profound changes take place, which explains why special instruments and methods are necessary to measure them.

THE SCENARIO METHOD

The scenario method, one of the most typical aspects of long-range forecasting, is designed to throw long-term light on decision-making in the context of a world of rapid change in certain fields. The re-search has a global nature and is concerned with the deliberate at-tainment of social goals determined explicitly and 'democratically', that is, through active co-operation among the participants in development.

In this method, the changes in a situation, a society or the international environment are forecast not by reference to the present situation but on the basis of a possible future scenario. An analysis is made of the potential or desirable factors of this scenario, which unfold in phases over a period of time and whose origins can be traced back to the present situation. Past and present trends are used as a starting-point for thought, not as unavoidable data which imprison the future within the confines of the present.[8]

Of course the aim is not to predict the future or programme it strictly on the basis of the data for the scenario or scenarios put forward, but to be able to use exploratory or anticipatory scenarios to infer what paths should be followed and what directions preferred and – an important aspect in the problems of interaction between culture and development – to make due allowance for the role of values and the notion of time when the scenarios are being worked on.

LONG-TERM DEVELOPMENT STUDIES

Taking the cultural factors into account in development also necessitates studying the long-term evolution of cultures and societies. Development problems at both national and international levels launched with the object of solving these problems cannot be fully evaluated in the short- or even medium-term perspective. In other words, discussing development means talking about the evolution of societies, changes in the world and in the course of history itself. Actions today have to be examined with the future in mind.

Long-term development studies are intended for that purpose. It will be remembered that in 1983, in response to the needs expressed by the African heads of state, the Economic Commission for Africa undertook a long-term study (1983–2000) of development in Africa. In late 1989, the World Bank published a similar study which outlined a strategic calendar for the continent. Finally, at a meeting held in Maastricht in 1990, the African ministers and

8. La Documentation Française, *La méthode des scénarios: travaux et recherches de prospective* [The Scenario Method: Futures Research], pp. 9–30, Paris, La Documentation Française, 1980.

international donors requested the African countries to prepare long-term national development studies with the aid of UNDP.[9]

Other studies of culture and development have been produced by UNESCO as part of its programme of long-range studies on the future of culture in Africa and Latin America, *inter alia*.[10] UNESCO has also published the proceedings of the Working Group on the Future of Culture, convened in 1990, and of the Tenth Conference of the World Futures Studies Federation on the future of development.[11] On another level the World Commission for Culture and Development has resolved to formulate long-range conclusions on development problems and trends in the twenty-first century which will spell out policy directions and, at least in broad terms, strategies and policies for both culture and development.

The desirability of a geography of cultural areas: an approach which needs to be explored

The compilation of a world atlas of cultural areas is both desirable and difficult. This visual presentation of cultural diversity would be a precious source of information for decision-makers on the different models, ways of life and thought, and beliefs in modes of social, economic and political organization which characterize the populations of a specific geographical zone. It could be a help in laying a geocultural foundation at different levels for the application of programmes which could be modulated to suit.

A task like this first of all raises the problem of the scale of the geographical zones defined and the significance of the cultural 'regularities' (or similarities) so plotted. It is of course possible to compile a map of major linguistic zones or geographical groupings which, for climatic, historical and economic reasons, have formed

9. Economic Commission for Africa, *A Long-term Study on Africa's Development*, Abidjan, UNDP, 1983.
10. World Bank, *Sub-Saharan Africa – from Crises to Sustainable Growth: A Long-term Prospective Study*, Washington, D.C., World Bank, 1989.
11. UNESCO, *The Futures of Culture*, Paris, UNESCO: Vol. I: *Meeting of the Working Group on the Futures of Culture*, 1991; Vol. II: *The Prospects for Africa and Latin America*, 1992.

regions in which common cultural traits exist. Examples are the Mediterranean basin and the Caribbean. One could also draw a map of the major population zones or areas with the same type of diet or culture. FAO has produced such a map of Africa.

The difficulty would lie in the choice of meaningful criteria (anthropological or institutional, for example) in relation to development problems or the identification of the principal traits of cultures to be found in the areas thus indicated. Another difficulty would lie in the very unequal availability of data enabling the cultures to be described in relation to the parts of the world concerned. Finally, an analysis would have to be made of the use to which this representation of the similarities and specific features of cultures in different parts of the world could be put, with a view to the creation of effective instruments to take account of the role of cultural factors in development.

It might perhaps be useful, by way of comparison, to see how the territorial boundaries are drawn for the application of the big development assistance programmes – or, conversely, how large quantities of data can be represented on very small geographical areas. Also it might be possible to devise a series of maps representing, individually or in small numbers, the cultural features of a given geographical area, which could be consulted one by one or by superimposition so as to arrive at a multi-criteria representation of the country or region for whose benefit modulated programmes would be drawn up.

CHAPTER 10

Instruments for work in the field

The instruments and methods just described relate first and foremost to the design and implementation of strategies, programmes and major projects with a general character because of their international or regional scale. Conversely, the methodological instruments which we shall look at now relate to work in the field, although there is some overlap with the previous instruments and methods.

Field operations which, by definition, require a detailed description of their implementation, must of necessity draw on specific instruments that are more sophisticated, both in their preparation and in their implementation and assessment. We shall therefore look in this order at: ways and means of defining cultural indicators of development; methods and conditions for project assessment; methods for evaluating the impact of projects; and ways of mobilizing local human and cultural resources.

Cultural indicators of development[1]

The questions that have to be examined in order to assess projects' cultural cohesiveness yield answers with varying degrees of accuracy. The compatibility of a project with the local culture has to be established by reference to a number of composite factors also

---

1. See X. Dupuis, *Contribution à l'étude des méthodes d'intégration des facteurs culturels dans le développement* [Contribution to the Study of Methods for Integrating Cultural Factors into Development], Paris, UNESCO, 1993.

called indicators. However, indicators useful to project heads or initiators will not necessarily be meaningful for the populations concerned, who may be prompted to work out their own ways of discerning the cultural effects of development by drawing on their own experience.[2]

Resources indicators in the development field are intended to: describe social situations; monitor progress and the reaching of objectives; make it easier to measure and understand social change; and analyse opportunities for comparison.

Unfortunately the indicators available at present for development projects are in most cases of an economic nature and there is no way of assessing the cultural dimension of development through national accounts systems. What is more, the cultural field is too heterogeneous and the cultural dimension of development too diffuse for it to be possible to construct arrays of indicators and statistical series that would be perfectly coherent, reliable and satisfactory. Again, in most developing countries national accounting is somewhat unreliable because of the scale of the informal sector of the economy and the weakness of the available statistical instruments. There is therefore no quantitative methodology of economic derivation that is sufficiently relevant to enable the cultural dimension of development to be taken into account.

This does not, however, mean that quantitative indicators are without interest for assessing the cultural dimension. Clearly, the evaluation of a project must include all the available and necessary information: economic indicators (role of the informal economy, propensity to consume or save, rate of inflation), demographic indicators (age pyramid, fertility, birth and death rates), health indicators (epidemiology), education indicators (facilities, numbers at school, number of graduates, literacy and enrolment rates) and cultural indicators (practices and facilities). However, it must be remembered that some of these indicators are still insufficiently sophisticated or accurate in the Third World and they can only be

2. See D. Goulet, 'Development Indicators Project: A Research and Policy Problem', *Journal of Socio-economics*, Autumn 1992.

estimated by long and costly fieldwork. The International Labour Organization (ILO), for example, has launched a large number of surveys to enable estimates to be made of the share of the informal sector in the economy of various countries.

The relationships between culture and society are highly complex and, alongside quantitative indicators which count and measure, we therefore also need qualitative indicators to identify differences, forms and forces (values, beliefs) and to ascertain their distribution, convergence or opposition in the social and cultural field. This means, therefore, coming up with qualitative indicators so as to identify the 'strategic' factors. Questionnaires already exist for the purpose, such as: the Framework for Cultural Analysis of the Asia Partnership for Human Development (APHD); the tables of 'criteria' or 'factors' like that of the International Centre for Bantu Civilizations (CICIBA) and of the Commission of the European Communities (cf. Part One); and lastly the 'Questionnaire for the Determination of Cultural Factors with a Bearing on Rural Development' and the 'Memorandum for Use by Technicians and Supervisory Staff in the Rural Environment' proposed by CICIBA. However, we must not lose sight of the fact that these factors can only be brought to light through the practical observation of behaviour patterns and attitudes in the field.

INDICATORS OF PERCEPTION AND TENSION

These indicators are used to assess the impact of the underlying, structural factors to which we drew attention in Part Two: beliefs, nature, and political, economic and social structures. These factors constitute the missing 'third dimension' which must be present in every development project. However, such broad factors are not in themselves sufficient, since they cannot be used for operational purposes in the decision-making process.

We must therefore look at the relationships with various components of development involving perceptions which, if they depart too far from those inherent in the economist's model, will simply be ignored.

The indicators proposed are composite and each of them may be taken to an extremely high degree of sophistication. Other definitions might thus be chosen by cross-linking or grouping together some of these indicators, given the close interactions that exist between them. They define the cultural dimension in broad strokes and, as presented here, are neither exhaustive nor definitive.

The indicators for beliefs and nature are as follows.

The relationship with time covers perception of the future and the role of history in collective representations. It is of course closely bound up with beliefs but it is also the result of the interaction with social inequalities: perception of and attitudes towards the future are partly conditioned by the precariousness of individuals' economic situations. The rate of progress of a development project may depend on this relationship with time, and the organization of the day and the seasons also plays an important role here.

The relationship with the environment covers the perception of nature as a set of abundant or scarce resources or a dominating or dominated environment. The management of the ecological heritage is directly dependent on this relationship with the environment – which also takes in the perception of space (limited/unlimited, rural/urban). This 'indicator' therefore provides an approach to different modes of life (sedentary or nomadic).

The relationship with the body and food includes both the perception of sickness and death (fatality-punishment/'accident of life') and attitudes towards fertility and taboos and customs in food and sexual matters. This connects it with the relationship to work (sexual distribution of labour) and the hierarchy (see below).

Another underlying factor, the *political, economic and social structures* of the group concerned, can be approached through three indicators.

The individual's relationship with the social group is the first of these. This embraces perception of the notion of identity (family/tribe/ethnic group/nation). It makes it possible to gauge the extent to which the capacity to mobilize a coherent social group matches up with the objectives of a project for that group.

The relationship with the hierarchy and power concerns the perception of what authority is based on in the group (process and power of decision within the group and *vis-à-vis* the outside). It therefore covers: the division between the sexes (role of women/men, distribution of roles in society as regards work and education), distribution by age, family relationship and birth (castes). This relationship determines human rights and duties but also, in interaction with individual/group relations (person-to-person

relations, links of authority or subordination, power distribution
in the family), relations between individuals and the administrative and political authorities (central and regional) and hierarchical relations in the world of work.

The relationship with the economy and innovation is inherently complex. It embraces the perception of money and goods (spending, saving, inherited assets, exchangeable goods, accumulated
goods), the perception of work (to survive, to grow richer, personal satisfaction, contribution to general effort) and its organization. In interaction with the relationship between the individual and the group and that with the hierarchy and authority,
it determines the form taken by business enterprise (informal/
formal or individual/family/community). The relationship with
innovation has to do with the question of techniques and know-
how (traditional and modern), risk and the advantage the population see in accepting or developing the innovation. It is decisive in the extent to which local energies can be mobilized.

How these criteria can be made operational

Using this checklist for the cultural cohesiveness of projects need
not systematically imply that a decision-maker has to embark on
long and costly research. Depending on the level of decision, the
degree of detail and accuracy required in the answers to the questions raised will vary. At the central level it may be sufficient, as is
already often done, to use global data and consult expert groups
and 'resource persons'.

On other occasions additional information may be required and
then field studies will be necessary, but they need not be expensive
if they can be fitted into the overall data-gathering process described
above (Part Two, Chapter 5).

Taking the cultural dimension into account by means of these
indicators will doubtless be more complicated for infrastructural
projects (roads, bridges, etc., for heavy transport, dams) and answering the questions involved will be the more difficult the closer
one comes to national integrated development policies, where the
issue of decentralized decision-making inevitably arises.

For projects on the regional scale, the difficulty is still greater
but it can sometimes be circumvented by having a large number of

187

tests at the micro level and picking out their common features.

Thus it is often easier to evaluate the factors at local level, or even in a given economic and social sector, by identifying their practical manifestations. Illustrations are the transition from subsistence to cash-crop farming, the informal economy, the industrialization process, modes of development of the urban habitat and the acquisition and maintenance of modern production plant, transport equipment and data dissemination facilities. Observing people's behaviour in these types of situation constitutes a basic feature of *ex ante* analysis.

Allowance will also need to be made for the interaction between these various phenomena, in particular by model-building (see Chapter 5). These interactions could be analysed, for example, between units of production, consumption and accumulation.

The production community should be consulted for obtaining facts about the creation of the product: working hours, growing techniques, and acceptability of operations to improve productivity. The consumer community should be chosen when the questions relate to phenomena to do with the workforce: food consumption, nutritional analysis, etc. Lastly, the accumulating community should be approached to evaluate economic surpluses and assets handed down (patrimony or matrimony).

Moreover, in the context of social development, it would be desirable to consider the relationship between these and other phenomena and aspects such as demographic policy (birth control), educational policy (with the various forms of education and training to be planned for), the status and role of women, and migration from the rural areas to the periphery of the big cities and to the most industrialized countries.

Thus these factors are relevant in the first instance to micro-projects, projects for community development or those targeted at groups such as minorities, women and young people. They are qualitative and can obviously not be expressed in figures. And although, at the global level, they may serve as the main headings for review by a group of experts and representatives of the population concerned at working meetings, their assessment in more refined terms must involve preliminary studies of the environment and qualitative studies on people's attitudes and behaviour.

A checklist for projects' cultural cohesiveness

At the macro-social level, i.e. that of central decision-making, culture is not directly operational: it contributes information on the cultural dimension in certain fields of social life. The problem for decision-makers is to determine the cultural dimensions they must address in order to minimize the risk of failure. What they want to know is whether, for the project they plan to mount, a cultural dynamic will or will not be generated socially for or against the project by those affected. It is true that part of the people's reaction will be of a cultural nature – but only a part and, as it happens, the part that is the most difficult to 'operationalize'. The rest will be a matter of the interests at work and what every player stands to lose or gain from the change.

The checklist here uses a five-stage iterative logic:

Phase 1. What form does the problem take? Documentary research and gathering of data.

Phase 2. What are the solutions to be applied? Formulation of project and definition of target groups.

Phase 3. Will the project be taken on board by the population? Check on receivability and acceptability of the project.

Phase 4. What are its effects going to be? Study of the project's foreseeable impact.

Phase 5. Finalization of project.

The project evaluator will need to pronounce on its validity at the end of each phase. The aim is to determine the cultural adhesiveness of a project and to bring out its degree of compatibility with the local culture and hence its adequacy for the needs of the populations concerned. It will ultimately be the decision-maker's task to assess the effectiveness of the project measured in terms of its cost, and not only its economic but also its cultural and social impact.

The economic, social and cultural effects can be closely allied, as the following example bears out. Originally of Buddhist inspiration, the Sarvodaya Shramadana movement (Gift of Work for the Ideal Society), which was founded in Sri Lanka, began in the form of a two-week work camp organized for the pupils of a higher Buddhist school by one of their teachers. The young people were sent out to remote and deprived villages to find out what the inhabitants needed and hoped for and to live with them, share their existence

189

and work at their side. In 1968 the originator of the experiment launched the project of the 100 villages which, with aid from Dutch and German donors, reached 2,000 villages in ten years, doubling these results by 1981.

For the Sarvodaya movement, development has no meaning unless it implies the full flowering of the human person, who does not stem solely from the production and consumption of material goods but also from the exercise of wisdom and compassion. The community development effort begins with a *shramadana* (gift of work) during which needs are identified and a project set in motion. Other projects are then decided upon and the Sarvodaya network supplies ideas, resources and technical and material assistance. The movement has an ecumenical basis, being active in Buddhist, Christian, Hindu and Muslim villages, and founds its development programme on the satisfaction of ten basic needs: water, food, housing, clothes, health care, communication, fuel, education, enjoyment of an attractive pollution- and danger-free environment and a spiritual and cultural life.

IDENTIFICATION OF PROBLEMS: DOCUMENTARY RESEARCH AND COLLECTION OF DATA

The first requirement is to identify the problems. In general the project, as defined, will be characterized by detailed technical cohesion resulting both from the research and from the application of its outcomes. As a function of this internal rationality, the problem will now have to be situated in relation to realities in the field. Here, documentary research and data collection in the field can play their full part.

The next task will be to assemble all the information, including that of earlier evaluation reports on projects previously implemented among the populations concerned and similar projects carried out in other contexts.

Data gathering will enable missing information to be filled in by means of field studies. These may be of the statistical kind; as we have seen, statistics in developing countries are often deficient. Secondly, some projects may call for information in areas where official data are lacking, for example, in the case of the informal sector.

Statistical data (economic, social or cultural) will sometimes need to be supplemented by quantitative data. Systems analysis (see

Chapter 9) could well be used here to bring out the structural elements that have to be taken into consideration.

DEFINITION OF THE PROJECT AND DETERMINATION OF THE TARGET POPULATIONS

Once the documentary phase has been completed, the necessary adjustments must be made to the project and, first and foremost, the populations concerned properly targeted. The object here is to arrive at a knowledge not only of the population's way of living, thinking and acting but also, as we have seen, of its needs as the people themselves perceive them. Above all, it is a matter of the feeling the population may have of its interests being understood, in an operation that is claimed to provide it with services or facilities of which it feels the need and which, as we have seen, will not necessarily be perceived uniformly as welcome or of no use by all members of the community. Here we come back to the problem of social division, even in small human groups as described in Part Two.

The second important point is, of course, the adjustment of the project, the broad outline of which may have been sketched out at an early stage on the basis of information gathered by the team of 'developers'. This adjustment exercise will be done very practically by discussion with the people who will play a particularly active – and indispensable – role in this phase of the project.

The project, therefore, cannot be finalized until a field analysis, the only way to provide the information necessary for cultural factors to be taken into account, has been drawn up. It also provides information that can be used for the later phases.

DETERMINATION OF THE RECEIVABILITY AND THE ACCEPTABILITY OF THE PROJECT

A knowledge of the local culture is essential in order to tell whether a project will be well received. However, a pragmatic assessment can be made of the receivability of a project as a function of the origin of the initiative (local/external), the consultation of local experts and the implication of the target groups. Clearly, a local initiative founded on consultation and effective participation of the groups concerned is unlikely to enter into direct conflict with local beliefs or structures. This phase can therefore be described by a sequence of simple questions. In practice, the problems of receivability and acceptability are closely related and if a distinction is drawn it is for logical convenience.

The receivability of a project may be determined by answering the following questions:

- What is the origin of the initiative (local or external)?
- Have experts been consulted? If so, who?
- Has the population been consulted and, if so, how?
- How are they going to be involved in the project?
- Has the population been involved in the formulation of the project and, if so, how?
- Is the project, at face value, receivable or could it well be rejected outright?

The acceptability of a project may be approached through a number of essential questions:

- What needs of the population concerned is the project designed to meet? Do they square with the consensual interests of the population?
- What motivations (better quality of life, progress, modernity, being better off) will be appealed to in order to mobilize the population?
- How will the project be presented and explained: by fieldworkers with the help of the media and educators, for example? How will the population be informed?
- On what techniques and structures will the project be based?
- If these techniques and structures are not endogenous, would it not be possible to employ local ones?
- In what way are the proposed techniques and structures preferable?
- How compatible are they with the local culture?
- To what extent is the local population attached to these local techniques and structures (impact of religious representations, relations at work, formal or informal sector, the economy)?
- On what conditions and within what amount of time could these techniques and structures be adopted by the population?
- Does the project appear to be acceptable or is there a risk that it could be rejected?

In Haiti, for example, a United States Agency for International Development (USAID) reafforestation project was unsuccessful until its design was changed as a result of social surveys and the consultation of beneficiaries. Previous forestry projects launched by the government or donors had failed. Even the thousands of saplings planted in the framework of the 'food for work' programmes by local peasants had been abandoned or sold for firewood. Social surveys showed that the prospect of long-term profits or the appeal to patriotism had not sufficiently motivated the people. A local-level project – USAID's Agroforestry Outreach Project – in 1981 succeeded because the peasants had been told they could regard the planted trees as a cash crop and left them free to plant them where they wished so that their own subsistence farming did not suffer. Supervision of the project was entrusted to NGOs that did not misuse the funds. The targets set were quickly achieved and some 110,000 Haitian peasants planted over 25 million trees between 1982 and 1986.[3]

Analysis of the foreseeable impact of the project

After clarifying the question of the degree of receivability and acceptability of the project, its foreseeable economic and sociocultural impact has to be assessed.

The economic impact – which is always taken into account – presents a number of methodological problems for which suitable instruments have already been designed and are widely used. The possibility of adapting them for use in studying the cultural impact of a development project needs to be examined.

In this regard, quantitative indicators can be used to assess the impact of a project. Various techniques could be used, for example, the 'effects method' (used in French co-operation projects), the 'reference price method' (used by the United Nations Organization for Industrial Development (UNIDO) but not analysed here) and lastly 'impact studies'. Here only the effects method and impact studies appear to be suitable for adaptation to qualitative problems.

The effects method is used to assess the social impact of a project over and above its economic aspect. When a decision-maker mounts a development project, he often seeks to measure its

3. See M. Cernea, *Putting People First: Sociological Variables in Rural Development*, Washington, D.C., World Bank/Oxford University Press, 1985.

economic viability in terms of its useful life and the population's degree of preference for its immediate or future benefits. However, this simple criterion is not sufficient to enable a decision to be taken because the decision-maker will also want to measure the project's impact on the whole of the community or country, which may mean having to take certain sociocultural aspects into account. The method is based on the effects of a redistribution of incomes and added value throughout the economy. It also enables projects to be classified and situations compared with the projects and without the projects. Dispensing with the detail, it may be said that this method is based on the principles of neoclassical economics. It seems particularly suitable for the developing countries as it enables rare factors to be assessed.[4]

As regards impact studies, it should be noted at the outset that they are not designed to take account of the cultural dimension of development. They can, however, be used to evaluate the impact of a project on a local economy. So an impact study cannot, directly, take the cultural impact into account, except to the extent to which the contribution of an economic project changes cultural attitudes.

Impact here is understood in a restrictive way and reflects the monetary implications of economic development. A calculation of the number of jobs created is often added. Three kinds of impact are distinguished:

- *the direct impact,* i.e. all the flows injected into the local economy by the activity concerned (wages, expenditure on goods and services, and tax revenue);
- *the indirect impact:* this represents the effects generated by the activity, i.e. all the spending on the project which will also be injected into the economy indirectly through the very fact of the project's existence;
- *the induced impact:* the businesses, households and even the public authorities which receive income associated with the direct and indirect impact of an activity reinject this income into the economy; this generates further activities and also has a fiscal impact (tax and equivalent deduction from earnings, tax on industrial and commercial profits, value added tax, etc.).

4. L. Augustin-Jean, *Contribution à la synthèse méthodologique sur l'intégration des facteurs culturels au développement* [Contribution to the Methodological Synopsis of the Integration of Cultural Factors in Development], pp. 8–9, Paris, UNESCO, 1993.

A broader assessment of the impact of the project should take account, over and above the quantitative indicators, of the qualitative and social and cultural components. It should also include a section on the future (for example, changes in the situation of women and in power relationships within the groups concerned).

In the first place there is a strong temptation to use cost-benefit analysis (CBA), whose purpose is to guide public decision-makers by telling them which is the best of a set of possible solutions at the collective level. CBA is widely applied in many different sectors: infrastructural projects, health and education policy, and so forth.

CBA is based on econometrics and therefore applies the general principle of monetarization.

The application of econometrics, however, is based on different binding assumptions which imply that all the factors to be considered must be quantifiable, that is, only quantifiable factors can be taken into account. The whole qualitative dimension is disregarded from the outset.

Cost-benefit analysis is therefore conditioned by its postulates and assumptions and appears ill-adapted to the inclusion of so vague a dimension as culture.

Another method of wide use as an aid to decision-making is cost-effectiveness analysis, which seems far more appropriate than CBA since it has been applied with some success in the sectors of health, education and the environment, where the qualitative dimension is vital.

The method consists in listing the costs relating to a project and confronting them with an array of indicators, enabling the overall effectiveness of the particular project to be evaluated. Where there is a choice between a number of projects, cost-effectiveness analysis provides decision-makers with comparative tables in which the different costs and outcomes of implementation of the different projects are expressed in their original units.

However, it is difficult to compare factors which are not directly comparable as they are expressed in different units. If the true significance of benefits and costs is to be retained, the need will obviously arise for a framework enabling a weighting to be assigned to each element and preference given to a particular project that will generate categories of benefits or minimize types of costs held to be more important than others.

The sociocultural impact can also be approached to some extent

195

by using quantitative indicators: death rates, morbidity rates, fertility, literacy, crime, etc. However, these indicators cannot reflect certain qualitative trends: changes in the status of women, in the foundations of ownership, in power relationships in the group and in religious practice and impact on the environment, and so on.

The overall assessment of the impact of a project must therefore include both quantitative and qualitative components. The decision will then be taken in the light of a global assessment of the positive and negative effects in a forward-looking framework, i.e. with a calendar of effects.

The cultural and economic impact of a project must also be the subject of an *ex post* evaluation when a given time has elapsed after completion of the project. Such studies have to be made by pluridisciplinary teams in order to measure all the changes brought about by the project. It is important to determine the impact of the project, in spite of the additional cost, not only for the project itself but also in relation to future projects.

In assessing the cultural dimension, all the partners involved at every stage of the project cycle must play a balanced role:

- at the identification phase, when it is a matter of translating demands and expectations into needs and development objectives;
- during preparation, ordinarily confined to the national administrative and technical officials, plus the experts and the financial executives;
- during project implementation;
- at the time of the evaluation processes.

Need for ongoing evaluation (monitoring)

An evaluation of the baseline situation is the vital point of departure which alone can enable the effects of the project to be assessed. This *ex ante* evaluation (which may take the form of a self-evaluation by the partners directly involved, i.e. the population, NGOs, agencies) provides an opportunity to compile and update the relevant data and develop a keener awareness among all the participants. From it a 'control board' should take shape, consisting of indicators and reference points which will enable these participants, and in particular the target groups, to make the project their own, steer it and make their own evaluation.

This first assessment must therefore help to:

- secure the involvement of the various decision-makers, authorities, institutions, organizations and companies that might have to act at project level;
- create awareness among the people and motivate and mobilize the populations concerned;
- identify and categorize local human and technical potential;
- look for any local structures that could be drawn on and choose appropriate technologies – whether local or from outside;
- formulate objectives and translate them in terms of expected impact;
- provide tolerances to ensure flexibility;
- make provision, as necessary, for a small-scale test of the project;
- encourage the formation of new work groups and teams at the different operational levels and strengthen those that exist.

This *ex ante* study will also enable the project's terms of reference and immediate goals to be defined, together with the products and the activities which will contribute to the attainment of these objectives.

Concomitant assessment tests out the instruments used for operating, regulating and managing the system (instrument arrays, indicators). It keeps in step with the progress of the project and is a decisive activity in plumbing the assumptions on which the action is based. It may therefore also possibly serve as an occasion to adjust and correct the directions being followed, i.e. the changes necessary because of empirical findings and changes of scale, in the way things go and in the attitudes and behaviour of the participants.

In this connection, a small-scale test will also enable a number of preliminary adjustments to be made and so limit the extent to which the project drifts off course.

The *ex post* evaluation is equally desirable and necessary. Its purpose is to draw up a balance sheet of the effectiveness and efficiency of the project by identifying the factors that have served as driving forces or obstacles to action. It will be a vital source of reference for future projects. It will clearly be the easier to draft and the richer in content the more the persons making the assessment find themselves in dialogue with partners of heightened awareness and enlightened by their active participation in the evaluation exercise from the outset.

Projects are sometimes met by strategies on the part of the population to misuse the resources, that is, to modify the projects to suit what the people perceive as their needs. Evaluation, therefore, must first and foremost be a permanent platform for observing social, cultural, economic and political realities. The fact that a project does not achieve its goals does not automatically imply that it has been a failure. Other – unexpected – effects may in fact have proved beneficial to the population 'misusing' the project perceived by them as an opportunity to pursue objectives they have felt to be more important.

Since *ex post* assessment generally comes quickly after the end of the activity, it naturally tends either to underestimate the long-term impact of the project, which may be considerably delayed, or to overestimate it because the deterioration of infrastructures (in the broad sense) or difficulties of depreciation are slow to become apparent. A project is not completed when assistance comes to an end of the timetable originally set. It spreads over a longer period of time. An evaluation should therefore include subsequent work to gauge medium- and long-term effects.

How local human and cultural resources can be mobilized

It goes without saying that the implementation of development projects should draw as far as possible on local potential. It avoids costly technology transfer and roots the project more strongly in the local context. The tools described above facilitate this process. Similarly the participation of the population (see Chapter 12) is more easily mobilized.

Although this is more easily achieved at the technical than at the human level there is generally a strong potential of local networks or organizations which can serve as the basis for originating or setting up projects.

However, this use of local networks – particularly those of an informal nature – is sometimes inhibited by the attitude of the local or regional authorities.

Also, some projects owe their success to the creation of structures requiring the stimulation of local energies. This has been done by setting up co-operatives, but the many failures in this area suggest a need for caution: the local culture and social organization must always be taken into consideration.

So it would be a good thing to give a greater role to the NGOs, which sometimes enjoy more trust from the local people than the authorities and official bodies. They could also play the part of intermediaries in reducing the gap which often divides the governed from those that govern them.

All this local potential is waiting to be tapped and ways of putting it to use should be part and parcel of evaluation methods.

CHAPTER 11

Multidisciplinary approach and creation of a cultural awareness of development

The need for a multidisciplinary approach based on experience

The emphasis placed in this work on the analysis of interactions and on the plurality of factors and participants in the development process obviously leads on to the proposal that a multidisciplinary approach should be adopted for working out the means of analysing the development situations that are to be influenced and for testing the working instruments arrived at in this way on 'full-scale' projects. That approach is an essential condition for integrated development.

The necessary descriptions must involve the social and human sciences in particular. It would be superfluous to stress the importance of the contribution which specialists such as historians, geographers, economists, sociologists, anthropologists, futurologists and others may make if the need arises. In some cases, multidisciplinary teams will have to be formed to work simultaneously; alternatively, specialists in the different disciplines will be called upon to take part in successive phases in the formulation, implementation or evaluation of projects.

Anthropologists have a decisive role because of their detailed knowledge of the cultural reality of traditional societies. An anthropological approach focused on persons and on specifics enables the realities of everyday life, habits and attitudes, tastes and preferences to be identified through raw documents and personal evidence. The anthropologist is able to put forward models which can reconcile the goals of development with traditional structures by emphasizing, for example, the need to exploit the authority of customary chiefs instead of marginalizing their role.

Far more sophisticated disciplines may also be used. For example, the semiological approach helps to throw light on facets which remain invisible to observers who are alien to the culture which is being studied. The aim will be to understand and associate the meanings and connotations carried by the facts and documents which are gathered. Here we are in the area of the language of symbols and signs of the group in question. Through the connotations of words in the particular culture, the study of languages can throw decisive light on interactive forms, etc. To preclude the development of misinterpretations and unexpected blockages, it is essential to understand how, and to what extent, apparent differences conceal still deeper resemblances and vice versa.

The second important observation that the preceding chapters have highlighted concerns the institutional distance separating field-workers from decision-makers in the major organizations providing aid to development. It is therefore important that the research and theoretical work of specialists should be linked with the practical experience of development workers who are in direct contact with the people, an approach that could be called experience-based.

The scientific expression of this approach is, in any case, to be seen in action-oriented research and the participatory survey. Action-oriented research could be defined as the combination of a field project with the concomitant analysis of the relationships that come into being between the people concerned (the public and the project workers), the factors involved in it, the stages of its implementation, its impact and the link that continues to exist, in the daily interplay of all these elements, between action and research and between those involved and those observing. In other words, the framework of the research is the execution of the projects themselves.

One might certainly think that there is only a difference of degree between action-oriented research and the participatory survey, since the agent is more directly involved in the latter method than in the former. The participatory survey implies that observers play a part in the action, that is, that they are accepted to the point of becoming members of the group and their observer status is almost forgotten, although they remain present as individuals. Observers act only to create the conditions which will enable the group to conduct the survey, although they are the ones who will draw conclusions from it. Observers must therefore remain neutral, not express any value judgements, offer their services if necessary and, in order to advance their work, listen rather than ask too many questions. It is understood that the conclusions of their work will be submitted to the group and discussed with it.

There is a third approach which is beginning to gain some importance and this is action-oriented research and training.[1] This implies a combination of research and action but also implies acceptance of the idea that any development moves include aspects of research, action and training. Beyond traditional scientific research, it implies that the researchers are involved in the functioning of the family, clan, village or neighbourhood, particularly in environments near towns. They are thus researchers, agents and training instructors all at the same time. In all three roles, they will have to bear in mind that they themselves have their own specific culture and experience whose validity is relative in comparison with the culture and experience that they are encountering.

This naturally means that over and above a training in the social and human sciences, communication or development methods, the researcher must, from the outset, be open-minded and receptive to other cultures and to the people of those cultures. These qualities can scarcely all be acquired through specialist training unless an intercultural approach is adopted, as will be seen in the following chapter. They are qualities which are part of the very personality of the fieldworker.

Finally, it is obvious that in this area, where the knowledge of experts comes into contact with the unique experience of people, the work done will alternate between theoretical considerations and the field, and in the latter case emphasis will be placed on action-oriented research and, above all, on the observation of the behaviour patterns and attitudes of people in their daily lives and the way in which they use their culture to solve the problems of improving their living conditions and, in some cases, ensuring their very survival.

1. See *Quid pro quo* (Brussels), No. 12, 1993, pp. 14–21.

Cultural training and awareness-creation among development leaders

Training and awareness-creation for decision-makers and development agents are a precondition for the changed approach needed if the cultural dimension of development is to be genuinely taken into account.

The juxtaposition of the two terms 'training' and 'awareness-creation' clearly demonstrates the complex educational implications of approaching development issues from a cultural standpoint, which does not merely consist in adding an extra component to the analysis of the factors conducive to development. Moreover, the use of the two terms implies, on the one hand, the acquisition of knowledge and know-how and, on the other, a change in the perception by those in charge of development at all levels, both of their own culture, including their professional and business culture, and of the culture of the societies or social groups on whose behalf action will need to be taken.

Such a change in perception may entail a change in the definition of the objectives of the project and the means of implementing it and, more broadly, a recognition of the importance in any living culture of emotional or irrational factors, or at least factors that obey a different kind of rationale from the modernist, technical and organizational rationale with its sights constantly set on optimum cost-effectiveness.

The organizations of the United Nations system have in fact already to some extent made allowance for the need for such training, at least at the stage of implementing and evaluating field projects. As we shall see later, UNESCO, for its part, has already carried out work in this area, both by devising models for specialist training and by organizing training and retraining courses and seminars for the personnel concerned. Bilateral co-operation agencies (Canadian International Development Agency, German Co-operation Agency, French Ministry of Co-operation) and some NGOs (such as OXFAM and the 'Cultures' network) have also set up their own systems for training personnel co-operating in and working on development projects.

The experience thus gained provides some of the answers to three crucial questions: Who should be trained (or made aware)? How should they be trained? To what end?

Multidisciplinary approach and creation
of a cultural awareness of development

THE PROPOSED TRAINEES

A short answer to the first question might be to say that all those involved in development must be convinced in one way or another of the importance of the cultural dimension of development and be prepared to act accordingly. As matters stand, the priority is to offer complementary training to external agents at all levels in the development process – decision-makers and scientific or technical specialists, both in institutional structures and in the field, and at both the international and the national levels.

Where the acquisition of knowledge and' know-how is concerned, it must be understood from the outset that the persons to be trained are adults, some of whom hold senior posts and can devote only a very little time to such activities. For this reason it is perhaps in the course of the initial training of future key personnel of national or international development agencies that disciplines relating to the 'soft' sciences should be introduced, together with practical field courses, on projects in which the specific features of the local context are very marked but do not constitute an insurmountable difficulty.

It was along these lines that UNESCO organized a series of meetings during the 1980s, aimed either at prompting heads of establishments for the training of senior civil servants, development agents or future specialists to consider introducing the human and social sciences into their curricula, or at confronting the future leaders themselves with real-life or simulated situations in which local cultures and development operations interacted. This experience yielded a number of conclusions from which broader inferences could be drawn for training and promoting the cultural awareness of those responsible for development.

But, as we have seen, it is not just a matter of passing on knowledge and know-how. The communication of theoretical specialist knowledge and even practical training courses, at least of the conventional kind, must go hand-in-hand with action to generate awareness among personnel responsible for development and other development agents. Organizing information seminars on the psychology, culture or attitudes of population groups will not be sufficient to induce development agents, now or in the future, to act more perspicaciously when it comes to improving the chances of success of the introduction of a technical innovation in a rural area, for example. The problem is in fact far more complex, for a number of reasons. It has to do with the very nature of cultural factors, which can be approached more satisfactorily from the standpoint of the human and social sciences. But these sciences are constrained by the 'formlessness', as it were, of culture and of human behaviour. Whereas it is easy to work on something that can be measured in rational or strategic terms, it is more difficult to pinpoint that very essential part of any culture, the symbolic and the imaginary. There is a 'powerlessness' here that scientists and field-workers have difficulty in accepting. Becoming aware of the cultural dimension of development amounts, in part, to accepting rationally the limits of scientific rationality and working on the basis of that acceptance. In other words, it means adopting a genuinely intercultural approach in apprehending and dealing with development issues.

OBJECTIVES AND CONTENT OF TRAINING

Training key development personnel in the cultural approach takes place at two very different levels. In what is termed intercultural management, it involves training business managers to grasp the psychology of economic or political leaders of other countries or the distinctive features of foreign markets. When it comes to training future development agents in the cultural approach to development, what they must be made to understand is the concept of integrated development and the special place of culture in such development.

Recent developments on the international economic scene which now make it impossible to manage national organizations or enterprises without taking account of the increasingly close interlinking of economies have latterly raised the question of training in intercultural management. The people who should receive such training are, on the one hand, those in charge of public development aid agencies and field agents and, on the other, heads of private sector enterprises working with partners belonging to different cultures.[2]

With the growing globalization of economic activities, the latter category of leaders are increasingly having to face up to the extreme

2. See the reviews *Entreprendre et former* (Paris), Nos. 1–2, June 1993, and *Education permanente* (Paris), No. 114, March 1993.

diversity of situations in which they operate. Seen from this standpoint, intercultural management is a set of strategies and management methods adapted to different cultural contexts. This is particularly true of multinational corporations, although a distinction must be drawn between three major categories of 'management cultures'. These may be either a reflection of the culture of the country of origin, or the result of a process of adjustment to other cultures, with all their differences, or, finally, the deliberate product of a multilateral firm's corporate culture. In these various cases, the method of training will consist in either 'expatriating' key personnel from the parent company who are able to adjust to different cultural contexts, or training within the parent company personnel from the countries in which the firm has established operations.

The first step is to inform the senior staff concerned by providing them with the keys that will make it easier to decode different forms of behaviour among their foreign partners, for instance as regards ways of communicating instructions, forms of motivation and methods of assessing results.

Learning about the appropriate action to take in an intercultural situation can be done through intercultural seminars for key personnel, which can either provide training of a conventional kind or focus more on active training methods, for example by explaining the difficulties of teamwork in working groups, or by simulating professional group situations in which cultural factors are brought into play.

Finally, learning about appropriate attitudes to take, i.e. learning to empathize, entails acquiring an ability to identify oneself with others, feel what they feel and internalize their cultural values so as to arrive at an understanding and a properly balanced relationship in intercultural contacts. The mere description of the aim and content of such learning clearly shows that what is needed here is a change of outlook, a radical transformation in the general attitude of the personnel concerned. Fieldwork – that is, close contact with the environment – can help to achieve this to some extent. Here, the most effective approach in principle would be the action-oriented research or participatory survey method. But if time is short, some recommend the 'culture-shock' approach, i.e. a brief period spent in a very different environment, which will at least enable the future leader to appreciate the scale of cultural differences.

ARE THERE ANY GENERAL RULES FOR CULTURAL TRAINING/AWARENESS-CREATION FOR DEVELOPMENT?

In general, it may be stated that the more specialized the expertise of the persons in charge of development, the greater will be the need to give them a broader vision of the sociocultural context in which they will have to work. Thus, the town planner, agronomist, engineer, administrator, economist and technician must first be made fully aware of the fact that other types of knowledge and expertise, other kinds of production or economic and social organization, other modes of thought or value systems predated those to which they themselves subscribe and continue to coexist with them. By taking full account of them in their approach to development problems and in their formulation of short-, medium- and long-term goals, they will be more likely successfully to implement projects whose economic, technical and administrative soundness cannot in itself guarantee success.[3]

Education in the cultural side of development is therefore essential in any endeavour to design and put in place cultural and intercultural training for the leaders of economic and social sectors. In this regard, it would no doubt be desirable to establish a wider, multidisciplinary basis for the training of future economic, administrative, scientific, technical and social decision-makers in areas such as health. In some sectors, such as the tourist industry, training which is not only technical and commercial, but also cultural, might be envisaged. In addition, the emphasis would be placed on experience in the field at every level of training. In this connection, useful lessons could no doubt be drawn from existing training programmes in the management of cultural projects.

This assumption gives rise to a number of more specific problems which have significant consequences for the type of training to be offered.[4]

3. See UNESCO, *Proceedings of the Seminar on the Incorporation of the Cultural Dimension into a Project for Integrated Local Development in Tunisia*, pp. 39–40, Paris, UNESCO, 1988. (UNESCO doc. CC/CSP/FCP/10.)

4. UNESCO, *Draft Training Programmes for High-level Decision-makers on the Cultural Dimension of Their Tasks*, Centre for Cultural Resources and Training (India), Paris, UNESCO, 1990. (UNESCO doc. CC/CSP/CP/03.)

Without going into detail, a number of principles and major guidelines can be formulated in regard to the content and methods of such training.

- Firstly, in face of the hyper-specialization of tasks and the search for increasingly sophisticated types of training, a humanist – or transverse – dimension should be introduced into every course of highly specialized training.
- With regard to the profile of 'new' decision-makers or technicians of development, this training should reconcile the demand for high-level experts with the need for cultural agents of development.
- There is also a real need to question the level (university, postgraduate) of such training and the framework (specialized or other institutions) in which it is to be given.
- Such training might include a common core and optional elements depending on the specialized training given to the future decision-makers in other areas, taking account, of course, of the sociocultural, economic and political context in which they will be called upon to work. It should also be designed to strike a balance between the acquisition of theoretical knowledge and practical experience, which would be provided in alternating but complementary sessions, concluding with the assumption of real or simulated responsibilities in a development project.
- This training should no doubt be followed up by refresher sessions.
- Training and awareness-creation in this area should, of course, be seen as complementary.
- In any event, the experience acquired in training of this kind already existing at the national and international levels could be taken into account.

The answers to these questions will vary depending on whether we are dealing with high-level decision-makers or fieldworkers, with long initial training or short intensive courses, including refresher programmes. However, the very diversity of the kinds of personnel to be trained also raises the problem of the content of training. Is it always essential to include in the programmes a 'common core' of knowledge, supplemented by optional elements adapted to the needs of the persons concerned (decision-makers or operators, the staff of large institutions or fieldworkers)? Needs in this area no doubt probably vary so widely that the purely theoretical part of the training may be seen as varying in its usefulness, depending on the level and nature of the knowledge already acquired.

Long, formal training must of course be envisaged but it is still more important to lay stress on all the training programmes of a non-formal type associated with projects and actions: training actions which are as participative and community-based as possible and targeted on a varied audience – supervisory and operational staff as well as the general population – as a function of needs and expectations. At the level of themes and content, particular attention should be given to the cultural and intercultural approach.

In regard to the administration of projects, the methods of training and awareness-creation for senior officials should focus on persuasion, advice and aids to decision-making. Three types of training should be introduced:

- for senior officials and decision-makers, additional information on systems approaches to permit a global approach to situations and actions, underlining the interrelation between participants and factors;
- for the benefit of all partners, simulation and alternate role play to gain a grasp of the real situation;
- for most partners, the development of an awareness of the nature of the strategies involved and of the interests of participants and, for foreign experts and representatives, of the reality of the intercultural situation.

IS THERE A NEED TO 'TRAIN' OR 'RAISE THE AWARENESS OF' THE PUBLIC?

Whatever form it takes, the training/awareness-raising of senior officials should not be the sole – and unilateral – form of education contained in a cultural approach to development. It should also involve the population groups concerned and, in more general terms, the general public as a whole, who must be supplied with information and, provided that the possibilities and limitations are clearly evaluated, with educational follow-up action.

Informing the general public, for example by setting up rural radio stations, is one of the best means of communication between the 'developers' and the 'developed'. More generally, at the national and international levels, it is essential to raise people's awareness by informing not only the population groups concerned, but also, at the international level, public opinion, whose mobilization – as has been seen in the case of the environment – may have a decisive impact on progress in including the cultural dimension in development.

As far as the population groups themselves are concerned, the question not only of their education in general, but more specifically of their education in political awareness, democracy and even economics and business management becomes less clear-cut when seen in terms of training. Does it come within the scope of popular education as such or could it be a more or less covert attempt at indoctrination by the existing authorities? The question needs to be raised.

In this situation it is for social workers, fieldworkers or local organizers to establish a process of dialogue and reciprocal education between the 'developers' and the 'developed', involving a clearer understanding by the population group of itself and of the outside agents of development, whether from within the country itself or from abroad (in particular NGOs), and a greater sense of awareness on the part of the outside agents themselves. In other words, it is only in a spirit of action-oriented research or, in broader terms, through participation, that an acceptable educational approach can emerge which takes account of the whole range of relationships growing up between population groups and 'developers'.

CHAPTER 12

Participation as a condition for consideration of the cultural dimension

If the existence of human rights is included among the components which go to make up a culture, the consultation of the populations concerned and their participation in development are an essential contributory factor in the success or failure of development projects. In accordance with the United Nations International Development Strategy 1991–2000, the participation of all, men and women alike, in the economic and political life of the country, that is, in the democratic functioning of the institutions and structures of government and administrations, is meant to take place at national level.

Furthermore, some researchers and fieldworkers, notably among non-governmental organizations, consider that effective participation by the population, in other words the democratic functioning of society, is the key to taking culture in the broad sense of the term into consideration in development.

Viewed in this light, participation at the local level cannot be fully understood unless it is placed in the context of broader geographical groupings, whether regional or national, and in relation to the existence of institutional structures at these different levels. This observation therefore implies, alongside the notion of participation, the further notions of consultation between populations and administrative authorities and the decentralization or even the proliferation of centres of decision-making.

A development action can only take root with the population if it is based on the existing situation, and if the changes brought about are clearly identified, and the procedures and pace of their introduction defined and evaluated accurately.

The 'developers' and the 'developed': the vital need for co-operation[1]

We must therefore first be familiar with the cultural practices, needs and aspirations of the population and incorporate these data into the terms of reference or 'specifications' of the projects. Specialists in the social and human sciences must accordingly be given their rightful place in the teams responsible for the design and implementation of a strategy or project. Their specific contribution, which is vital from the standpoint of the respect due to the culture of any human community, is no less necessary with a view to operational effectiveness. Finally, and especially in local development operations, the working methods employed will be those of a participative survey and action-research: observations will be made in the field of the activities which are carried out and in an ongoing dialogue with the population on a basis of equal status in the negotiations; at the same time, the cultural profile of the 'developer' must be relativized.

But participation can go still further than this. As we have seen, the expertise of specialists is not in itself enough in any development project. There is a vital need to structure, using procedures which remain to be defined, the activity of the officials in charge around the creativity of individuals and groups and to encourage their participation in every possible way in the decision-making process and in the implementation and evaluation of every development action. In some instances, a sociocultural educational approach may be necessary to stimulate this creativity; the project leader must not be allowed to take over from the population concerned with his own intervention replacing the immediate truth of daily experience.

In the most favourable of cases, the population itself, either as a community or through spokespersons appointed by the group, will discuss its own situation, identify critical issues and priority problems, articulate its needs in more or less explicit terms and take the initiative when action is needed.

1. See H. Panhuys, E. Sizoo and T. Verhelst, *La prise en compte des facteurs culturels dans les projets de développement* [Taking Cultural Factors into Account in Development Programmes], Part 2: *Prise en compte des approches culturelles par les grandes agences de développement* [Acknowledgement of Cultural Approaches by the Leading Development Agencies], Paris, UNESCO, 1993. (UNESCO doc. CLT-93/WS/3.)

If a dynamic process of this kind develops, the outside members of the team must in their turn become active participants. They may be local leaders who have received the necessary training – as short and flexible as possible – or observer-participants engaged in fieldwork. Whatever the case, their role will consist in recording the opinions and knowledge that are expressed, or the shortcomings that are pinpointed, and in providing the necessary support, generally in the form of information or assistance in clarifying poorly formulated viewpoints or complaints. The situations may be highlighted by a dramatic presentation, simulated or spontaneous, of the different points of view, provided that the group dynamic created as a result can be kept under control.

Participation can be facilitated, as already pointed out, through broadly based information of the population. Every intervention and action must be explained at many different levels and by many different means, including the media. One of the obstacles to development is the poor circulation of information between the participants and misinterpretation by them. Allowance for the cultural factors in projects corresponds to an effort to translate (coding/decoding) the language of the basic groups in their villages or districts into the language of technical and administrative action.

Knowledge of the modes, circuits and centres of communication is therefore vital. Any reductive and distorting effects of the messages which are transmitted must be avoided as far as possible. The preparation of these messages in any case requires great experience and an excellent knowledge of the environment concerned. Here the mediators in the field have a decisive role to play: they must persuade and motivate the beneficiary groups to participate in properly understood actions.

But the effective implementation of participation poses a series of complex questions and raises problems of approach and methods of communication which can only in part be expressed in pre-existing bodies of expertise and are dependent as much on attitudes as on aptitudes.

Conditions for effective participation by the population

More than familiarity with the culture of the population groups which are to benefit from a development action is needed in order to persuade them to accept the projects proposed to them.

Clearly, any such acceptance, and the active dialogue and dynamic arising out of it, will have a scope and strength that vary widely with the type of project.

In the case of projects designed and implemented without reference to the population, even though the cultural factors adduced in any sound scientific study are taken into account, or if the population is merely invited after the event to collaborate in or at least not to obstruct the project, the rate of participation, using that term in its true sense, will be limited or even nil. Any action planned throughout in that way will thus have little chance of success.

In the case of projects that have been 'sold' to the population but were designed and 'granted' from outside to meet needs and solve problems identified without reference to the population, participation will be conditional and relative only. The population will not perceive them as a response to objectively determined needs, but in the light of its own interests as it itself sees them. Consequently, objectively useful projects may fail precisely because they have not brought about a genuine mobilization of the would-be beneficiary population.

Consultation and sustained dialogue with local communities are the best ways of stimulating the kind of demand that will make it possible to formulate, step by step, a project with which the population will identify, and in which it will therefore participate to the full.

DRAWING ON LOCAL CULTURES

Local cultures must be the foundation of any project. It must be recognized that a genuine dialogue between the 'developers' and 'developed' may result in an amendment of the decisions to be taken, once the strategies, interests and stakes as they are perceived by the 'developed' beneficiaries become known. We must also learn to consider opposition which reveals the conflict and antagonisms that underlie the power relations involved. Dialogue and participation are two preconditions for the success of the actions undertaken.

A human community can preserve the essential values of its identity and cultural integrity by modifying the social context to improve its quality of life. Traditional beliefs and practices are therefore not always a brake on economic growth. They may even become driving forces. Thus, many studies prove that the extended family can serve as a dynamic factor.

The answer therefore consists in treating cultures as cultural problem-solving models, as non-static models which may apply both to tradition and to modernity. Although cultural blockages are sometimes important – a fact which must not be disregarded – they cannot and must not be allowed to become insurmountable obstacles. Traditions nourish culture and are sufficiently permeable and malleable to adapt in the context of the essential mobilization of human resources. Such crucial issues for the developing countries as demography and the status of women can be resolved without entering into open conflict with cultural taboos.

Provided that negotiation and consensus-building are used and that sensitivities are respected, a solution which falls within the ambit of the cultural dynamic can always be arrived at. Of course, such a solution will rarely be reached in the short term, but prudence is a guarantee of the viability of any project. Precipitation is always a source of friction, not to say conflict, and hence of failure. In Morocco, for instance, participation based on existing groups has developed in a rather unusual way. The experiment, begun in 1963, is centred on the cultivation and pruning of olive trees and the marketing of the olives. It is a pre-cooperative project, and participants are recruited on a voluntary basis. Forty-two groups with 872 members in all were quickly set up. The groups are organized at the level of the *douar* (division for rural administration) and *adem*, village districts constituting the basic geosocial units of the tribal structure.

Results have been very encouraging and the organizations backing the project (the Moroccan National Office for Irrigation and IRAMD, a private French body) have been able to demonstrate the value of tapping local potential. Incidentally, one of the reasons why this association has been so successful is that the extension work was carried out with the help of local groups, taking advantage of local agricultural know-how.[2]

2. Panhuys et al., op. cit.

LISTENING TO THE PEOPLE AND AROUSING THEIR INTEREST

The second fundamental rule for any development action founded on participation is to promote self-expression by the population on the specific project and to discern the factors which arouse their genuine interest in the proposed actions. A key distinction must be drawn here between needs and interests. The notion of need – in any population, regardless of its economic, social and political context – is blurred and ambiguous. It is always hard to explain something which people do not possess or with which they are not familiar. On the other hand, individuals will always react positively to an external proposal if they are interested in it. The existence of the need is not enough. The interests involved reveal the power relations within the group and a need may involve divergent interests by calling into question social structures and relationships of authority (see Chapter 5).

The concept of interest also deserves to be considered from another angle. For example, UNDP-funded projects necessarily involve a corresponding input, in the form of activities or financing, by the local partners in the project. In general, a matching financial contribution is out of the question in the case of local development projects. However, it is possible to involve the population in the project by organizing activities which contribute to its implementation. The interest of the beneficiary community may thus be sharpened by the efforts and sacrifices that it makes to ensure that the project runs smoothly: this phenomenon is surely a concrete manifestation, and indeed an important indicator, of the degree of mobilization of the population: in other words, of its active participation in its own development.

Only an interest based on consensus will permit effective mobilization of the group. That is why population groups sometimes adopt strategies of dissimulation and seem to confuse the issue in order to protect themselves against external encroachment, preserve their own security and absorb external contributions as a function of their own specific internal mechanisms and rationalities. This accounts for misunderstandings and ambiguities between development agents and the population. The need here is therefore for genuine training in the creation of interest.

Effective participation by the population groups must then be obtained through information meetings and media coverage of projects. The population must be taught to listen; that is the only way of enabling projects to be perceived as issuing directly from local initiatives.

PARTICIPATION AND INSTITUTIONAL ACTION

However, participation often runs up against limits when it goes beyond the local level. Many micro-projects, arising from different situations and the strategies of many participants, cannot be accepted by the central authorities in every sector or beyond certain limits which vary according to the country and situation. There can be no doubt that making allowances for cultural realities through a geography of coherent cultural areas (or social territories) may make it possible to revert to traditional or even ethnic structures, which are sometimes better adapted to the local reality than modern methods of organization, which have their roots in the colonial history of some developing countries.

Participation by the local population in development projects can scarcely be achieved unless the governments have themselves defined the conditions for an effective participation policy. No doubt a *modus vivendi* will have to be found in each case in the light of the local context. The participation of the population can be gained on a lasting basis only by solving the problems experienced by some countries in the management of their public affairs or by developing a public service culture in order to strengthen mutual trust between the authorities and the population as the basis for any commitment by the latter to the development of the society to which they belong.

No doubt the notion of participation as such, and more particularly the conditions under which participation can become a reality, raise complex questions to which it has been possible to give only brief consideration here. There has at least been an attempt to bring out their most salient aspects. These questions still need to be examined thoroughly and, above all, conclusions need to be drawn for the work of all those involved in activities at the 'grass-roots' level. It is precisely with that aim in mind that, as part of the ongoing efforts to produce a clear outline of methodology, a 'practical guide for fieldworkers' is to be drawn up.

219

Towards a practical approach

Now that the three stages just covered in this inquiry have been completed, it is essential to review the situation in terms both of the primary goal of the World Decade for Cultural Development and of the place which this document occupies in the overall context of the 'Cultural Dimension of Development' project, as described in the detailed work plan adopted by the expert group which UNESCO appointed to follow up this project.

When we come to the World Decade for Cultural Development and its primary goal – which is regarded in some quarters as its only goal – the methodological overview approach can be said to represent a considerable step forward. This does not mean that the institutions of the United Nations system have not recognized, under a variety of names, the scientific and ethical need to incorporate aspects of development other than those relating to strictly economic, technical and organizational factors into their thinking and action. Some of them have even gone much further and have taken up some of the broader cultural aspects of development issues and activities. In some respects, they have even outstripped the efforts made by UNESCO, which has been unable to sustain the same pace, for lack of financial and scientific resources. This is true, for example, of the World Bank, UNICEF and UNFPA.

However, the actual thinking behind the Decade is such that it involves all the institutions of the United Nations system and the United Nations itself. Even so, this inter-agency approach has not generated as much impetus as might have been hoped. Many joint projects have already been carried out between UNESCO and such institutions as UNDP, the World Bank, UNFPA and FAO. However, the findings of some of these institutions as they pertain, for example, to rural development, administration, health, child care and education itself, have not necessarily benefited all the others. Yet these are areas where the Decade's primary goal is particularly important. In this respect, the synoptic report produced by UNESCO is an acknowledgement of the fact that there has already been considerable forward movement. In view of the very scope of the issues it raises and the effort it makes to systematize the data, analyses and possible solutions, the report makes a major contribution to the action carried out by the international and national governmental and non-governmental institutions, which are the partners that are constantly cited as being instrumental in the Decade's success. In a sense, the synoptic report could be said to represent a significant step in the formulation of a body of doctrine common to all the development institutions in the United Nations system. Further proof of this should be furnished by the subsequent stages in the 'Cultural Dimension of Development' project.

It is in this respect that it is important to pinpoint the work accomplished in terms of the project as a whole.

In the first place, it should be remembered that the methodological work proper has not yet been completed. Among other things, this accounts for the fact that discussion of policy planning and development project methods and instruments, training in the cultural approach of officials in charge of development, and above all the actual participation of the population in their own development still occupy a relatively limited place in the third part of the report. The second phase of the project, scheduled for the 1994–95 biennium, provides for the preparation and publication of a *Technical Manual for Planners* and a *Practical Guide for Development Field Workers*. These two publications will be a natural adjunct to the initial working aid represented by this synoptic report.

Needless to say, the ideas put forward in this document will be recapitulated, enlarged upon, gone into more deeply, added to, and borne out by examples, so that the two publications planned will prove to be really practical working aids for prospective users. In addition, in so far as it proves possible to test the methodological proposals contained in the synoptic report on actual development projects, especially with respect to the timing of activities, the findings of the observations made will be incorporated into both the manual and the guide, in order to make these more relevant and enhance their practical value.

Even so, a distinction must be made between the two publications. The proposals contained in the third part of the synoptic report relating to the revision of planning methods and the use of decision-making aids will require the strictest scientific follow-up if the aim is to ensure that the manual is of a high standard. Conversely, the direct observations made by local development agents and the experience they gain will add to the substance of the guide and will ensure that it has an impact based on real-life events.

The explicit purpose of the project observations made both by social and human science specialists and by development agents in direct contact with the population will also be to put the proposals contained in the present text to the test.

All this goes to show the importance attached to observer missions and, prior to that, to the selection of projects that will be subjected to specialist analysis. These projects should differ in scope (i.e. should include interregional, regional, national and local projects) and should cover a variety of economic, social, rural, urban, educational, health, population and other similar sectors managed by states, non-governmental organizations and intergovernmental organizations. In addition, wherever possible, action-oriented research and participatory survey techniques will be employed and as much use will be made of practical experience as of academic knowledge, if not more.

Another major problem is that of training development officials and agents. While due account will be taken of the knowledge already gained in this area, trials will also have to be conducted in order to gauge the merits of each type of training more closely; in other words, to determine whether provision should be made for initial or in-service training, with a cognitive or operational emphasis, designed for outside operators or local personnel, or even for the population itself in some instances.

In any event, all these activities should cater for a need which has been identified by all kinds of specialists at all levels and in all areas. The goal should be to move steadily in the direction of field-work and to involve the population more and more in responsibility for its own development. The question is whether, as stated at the beginning of the third part, this should be regarded as the start of a shift in outlook, in which development problems are approached through cultural realities rather than vice versa. The resulting changes would be far-reaching. The first of these would be the change in the direction of the initial drive imparted to development, whereby a series of small projects would be grouped together into larger and larger units, right up to the level of the decision-making bodies of the major organizations. From this point of view, the function of those institutions would be, firstly, to put some broad order into the budgetary and human resources required, so that they would be geared to the most appropriate level and, secondly, to situate these small- or medium-sized actions or sets of actions in the framework of major economic, political or cultural trends at regional or world levels and to set them in a long-term development perspective, so that the cultural relevance of the projects would be gauged in terms of the diversity of the specific contexts. This could perhaps be a useful pointer for attempts to 'marry' the outlook and action of the major organizations with real-life situations.

Bibliography

CANADIAN INTERNATIONAL DEVELOPMENT AGENCY. *Le développement durable* [Sustainable Development]. Hull (Canada), CIDA, 1991. (Position paper.)

——. *Social and Community Development.* Hull (Canada), CIDA, 1991. (Briefing paper.)

CLAXTON, M. *The Cultural Dimension of Development.* Paris, UNESCO, 1994. (UNESCO doc. CLT/DEC/PRO-94/01.)

CLERGERIE, B. *Dimension culturelle et processus de décision dans les entreprises et projets de développement* [The Cultural Dimension and Decision-making Processes in Development Undertakings and Projects]. Paris, UNESCO, 1993.

COMITÉ CATHOLIQUE CONTRE LA FAIM ET POUR LE DÉVELOPPEMENT. *Les mains ouvertes.* Paris, 1992. (1992 report.)

CULTURES NETWORK. *Quid pro quo* (Brussels), Nos. 8–14, 1992–93. (French only.)

Employment, Growth and Basic Needs: A One-World Problem (World Conference on Employment, Income, Distribution and Social Progress, and the International Division of Labour). Geneva, ILO, 1976.

MASINI, E. *The Cultures of Development.* Paris, UNESCO, 1991.

MORRISON, C. *Economics, Culture and Development* (Proceedings of the Symposium of International Catholic Organizations, 8–10 September 1992), pp. 52-60. Geneva, OECD Development Centre/ICO, 1993.

Our Common Future: The World Commission on Environment and Development. Oxford, Oxford University Press, 1987.

OXFAM. *Working for a World, 1992–1993.* London, OXFAM, 1993.

225

——. *OXFAM and Work Overseas*, 1992–1993. London, OXFAM, 1993.

PANOS INSTITUTE. *At the Desert's Edge.* London, 1991.

——. *Listening for a Change.* London, 1992.

SALMEN, L. *Beneficiary Assessment: Bringing Culture into Development* (Meeting of Experts on the Cultural Dimension of Development). Paris, UNESCO, 1991. (UNESCO doc. CC.91/Conf.602.)

UNDP. *Human Development Report.* New York, UNDP/Economica, 1990, 1991, 1992, 1993.

UNESCO. *Meeting of Experts on the Cultural Dimension of Development.* Paris, UNESCO, 1991. (Working document.)

UNICEF. *Regional Seminar on the Cultural Dimension of Development in Africa.* UNESCO/World Bank/UNICEF, 1992. (Working document.)

UNITED NATIONS. *International Development Strategy for the United Nations Development Decade.* New York, United Nations, 1970, 1980, 1990.

List of agencies consulted

1. Institutions and agencies of the United Nations system

- United Nations (UN)
- Joint Inspection Unit of the United Nations (JIU)
- United Nations Conference on Environment and Development (UNCED)
- United Nations Children's Fund (UNICEF)
- United Nations Conference on Trade and Development (UNCTAD)
- United Nations Development Programme (UNDP)
  - Planning and Co-ordination Office
  - Bureau for Programme Policy and Evaluation
- United Nations Environment Programme (UNEP)
- United Nations Fund for Population Activities (UNFPA)
- United Nations Institute for Training and Research (UNITAR)
- United Nations University (UNU)
- World Food Programme (WFP)
- Economic Commission for Africa (ECA)
- Economic Commission for Europe (ECE)
- Economic and Social Commission for Asia and the Pacific (ESCAP)
- Economic Commission for Latin America and the Caribbean (ECLAC)
- Economic and Social Commission for Western Asia (ESCWA)
- United Nations Centre for Human Settlements (HABITAT)
- International Research and Training Institute for the Advancement of Women (INSTRAW)

- United Nations Research Institute for Social Development (UNRISD)
- International Labour Office (ILO)
- Food and Agriculture Organization of the United Nations (FAO)
- World Health Organization (WHO)
- World Bank/International Finance Corporation (IFC)
- International Monetary Fund (IMF)
- World Intellectual Property Organization (WIPO)
- International Fund for Agricultural Development (IFAD)
- United Nations Industrial Development Organization (UNIDO)
- World Tourism Organization (WTO)

2. Multilateral co-operation

- Commission of the European Communities (CEC)
- Organization for Economic Co-operation and Development (OECD)
- Council of Europe (CE)

3. Bilateral co-operation

- Canadian International Development Agency (CIDA)
- Swedish International Development Agency (SIDA)
- Danish International Development Agency (DANIDA)
- Finnish International Development Agency (FINNIDA)
- Norwegian Agency for International Development (NORAD)
- Ministry for Co-operation (BMZ) (Germany)
- Ministry for Co-operation and Development (France)

4. Non-governmental organizations

RESEARCH AGENCIES AND NETWORKS

- European Association of Development Research and Training Institutes (EADI)

- Association of Asian Social Science Research Councils (AASSREC) (New Delhi)
- Association of Development Research and Training Institutes of Asia and the Pacific (ADIPA) (Kuala Lumpur)
- Association of Arab Institutes and Centres for Economic and Social Research (AICARDES)
- Council for the Development of Economic and Social Research in Africa (CODESRIA)
- Latin American Social Science Council (CLACSO)
- Graduate Institute of Development Studies (Geneva)
- Institute of Quantitative Economics (Tunis)
- Institute for Development and International Relations (IRMO) (Zagreb)
- International Co-operative Research Association (Paris)
- 'Cultures' Network (Brussels)

OPERATIONAL BODIES AND NETWORKS

- Conference of International Catholic Organizations (Geneva)
- Catholic Committee against Hunger and for Development (CCHD) (Paris)
- Oxford Committee for Famine Relief (OXFAM) (Oxford)
- Panos Institute (London)
- Association de la Nouvelle Économie Fraternelle (NEF) (New Fraternal Economy Association) (Paris)